The Young Atheist's Survival Guide

The Young Atheist's Survival Guide

Helping Secular Students Thrive

Hemant Mehta

Patheos Press | Englewood, CO

1st edition
Published by Patheos Press
Englewood, Colorado

12 13 14 15 16 17 18 19 20 21—10 9 8 7 6 5 4 3 2 1

Cover design by Jenny Ashford
www.jennyashford.com

Library of Congress Cataloging-in-Publication Data

Mehta, Hemant.
   The Young Atheist's Survival Guide: Helping Secular Students Thrive
   Includes bibliographical references.
   ISBN: 978-1-939221-07-0 (alk. paper)

PRINTED IN THE UNITED STATES OF AMERICA

Permission to use the speech reprinted in the Appendix was granted by Edwin Kagin.

For information, contact Patheos Press, 383 Inverness Parkway, Suite 260, Englewood CO 80112, or find us online at www.patheos.com/Books/Patheos-Press.

For Courtney

Contents
Acknowledgments

1: The Outcasts: *The Backlash against Young Atheists*

2: Taking Attendance: *How Many Young Atheists Are There?*

3: The Principal's Office: *When Administrators Attack*

4: Peer Pressure: *Dealing with Friends and Family Members*

5: The Morning Bell: *How Religion is Pushed into Public Schools*

6: Homework: *What Atheists Can Do to Make a Difference*

7: Curriculum: *Ways to Spread Friendly Atheism*

8: The PTA: *How Parents, Teachers, and Administrators Can Help Young Atheists*

9: Graduation: *Where We Go from Here*

Epilogue

Appendix: *"Thoughts For Atheists at Graduation"*

Resources

Notes

Acknowledgments

Over a decade ago, I saw August Brunsman give a talk about the Secular Student Alliance at a conference in Florida. I knew from that moment that I had to be a part of this movement. A friend once described August as someone who turned a "part-time hobby into a full-time career" and it's that sort of dedication to this cause that has inspired so many of us fortunate enough to work with him over the years. I also want to thank his team at the Secular Student Alliance, including Lyz Liddell, Jesse Galef, and Ashley Paramore for all they do to support young atheists.

This is not a book that many publishers would take a chance on, but the great staff at Patheos has championed both this book and the Friendly Atheist website and I can't express my gratitude enough. Many thanks to Leo and Cathie Brunnick, Dan Welch, Patton Dodd, and Kathleen Mulhern. Jana Riess took this book past the finish line and her questions helped clarify and strengthen several of my arguments.

As I mention in this book, many atheist teachers have a tough time at work, not because they express their religious views at school, but because they're atheists, period. I'm fortunate that it's not a problem I have to deal with thanks to an administration that cares about what I teach my students, not about what I write in my spare time. My colleagues, too, never let our religious differences get in the way of our friendships. Thanks to Vanessa Liveris and Jose Zaragoza for their constant support.

Andrew Seidel, Debbie Goddard, JT Eberhard, David Niose, Jamie Bernstein, John Mueller, Charlotte Abney, Todd Unger, Casey Smirniotopoulos, Richard Wade, and Michelle La Scola all offered incredibly helpful insights throughout this process.

My family has supported the work I do even when it's not easy for them to do so; many atheists are not that lucky.

Finally, I extend a tremendous debt of gratitude to all the students who were willing to speak to me on and off the record for this book. They have fought the status quo when it comes to religion and many have paid a price for it. Still, the fact that they challenge their friends, classmates, family members, teachers, administrators, and communities is inspirational. If they can do it, so can the rest of us.

1

The Outcasts

The Backlash against Young Atheists

When Nicole Smalkowski's family moved to an eighty-acre ranch in Hardesty, Oklahoma, a small town with a triple-digit population, making friends should have been the least of her concerns. She was an athlete, after all, and when you're thirteen, playing on a sports team is supposed to be a guaranteed way to meet new people. In the fall, Nicole made the football team at Hardesty High School—she was the only female on the roster—and she said the boys accepted her as one of their own.[1] A few months later, her spirits high from that experience, she tried out for and made the girls' basketball team.

On Friday, November 19, 2004, when the final buzzer sounded on the basketball team's first game, instead of shaking hands with opposing team members and saying "good game," all the players on both teams came together and joined hands in a circle at center court. They, along with the referees, the coaches, and the spectators, all bowed their heads and began to recite the Lord's Prayer. It was a tradition that caught Nicole off-guard.

As an atheist, Nicole had no intention of reciting the prayer. It wasn't just because of her personal disagreement with it, but also out of respect to the other students:

> I wouldn't do it because it's disrespectful to me. I think it's disrespectful to them [too]. Why would they want an atheist in their circle saying the Lord's Prayer? I mean, if I was a Jew or Muslim or Hindu, I would have a problem with that prayer.[2]

Coach Ernest Cook urged Nicole to join the circle, but Nicole told him that she didn't believe in God. Exasperated, he told her, "Go to the locker room then."[3] The incident should have ended there, but Coach Cook felt like this "situation" warranted further discussion. So the next day he got together with district Superintendent David Davidson and Principal Lloyd Buckley. It was apparent to them that Nicole needed to be punished for her disobedience. So the decision was made: she would be kicked off the team.[4] Making matters worse, none of the adults even had the decency to tell Nicole to her face that she could no longer play. She would have to figure that out on her own.

The following Tuesday, when Nicole looked at the roster for the team's next game, her name was nowhere in sight. Was it a mistake? Would she play in the following game? Would she play at all for the rest of the season? The answer to all of those questions was a definitive "no." Nicole was baffled. *What had she done wrong?* When she asked her coach for a reason, his response confused her even more: She was being punished for stealing another student's sneakers and lowering team morale.[5]

Of course, Nicole had never stolen any sneakers from anybody. She said she had *borrowed* sneakers from a teammate but later returned them (witnesses even saw the exchange). Furthermore, how could she have lowered team morale when she came to practices *early* to run laps?

Still, once the allegations went public, it was hard to stop other rumors about her from spreading. People found all sorts of reasons to pick on her, the least of which was the supposed theft. Many of the accusations revolved around her atheism. Nicole was harassed about her religious and political views by both students *and teachers* over the next few days. Students called her a "devil worshiper."[6] They called her "gay" because she had said she supported Democrat John Kerry in that year's presidential election.[7] They called her a "half breed" because of her parents' mixed ancestry. The principal's son told her he wanted to grab a gun at the very sight of her.[8] Teachers told her they hated her, that it was a Christian country, and that she could get out if she didn't like it.[9] The teachers were fully aware of what the students were saying about Nicole, but they did nothing to stop it. Later, when talking about what happened to his daughter, Nicole's father said the harassment amounted to dealing with a "religious gang."[10]

After her family objected to the accusation of theft, a lawyer for the school district admitted that Nicole's "lack of participation in the team's religious ceremony" was one of the factors that led to her being kicked off the team.[11]

One year later, Nicole was allowed back onto the basketball team. It is a testament to her own tenacity that she was even willing to return.

On Friday, November 18, 2005, nearly a year to the day since her last game, it happened again.

At the end of the game, another prayer circle formed at center court—that practice hadn't changed from the previous year. In a short video Nicole posted online, you can see the black uniforms of the opposing team on the left half of the circle.[12] On the right half are the white uniforms of the Hardesty High School team. And then, a little further to the right, you can see Nicole standing alone outside the circle in a white uniform, her hand on her heart, reciting the Pledge of Allegiance (sans "under God"). Afterward, a teammate gives Nicole a hug and whispers something in her ear. According to Nicole, that student told her, "God forgives you, and I forgive you."

The following Monday, Nicole was kicked off the team for the second time. She was accused of threatening to kill another player on the team. She wasn't given a chance to defend herself against the accusation.

Nicole and her family ultimately decided this was all too much to bear. Though she could easily have been eligible for an athletic scholarship down the road given her talent, this just wasn't worth it. Nicole's father took her and her younger siblings out of the public school system in Hardesty and began to homeschool them.

A year into her homeschooling, Nicole was in tears as she recalled how little had changed since she left Hardesty High:

I miss school... but I don't wanna go back to that
school. I tried going back to that school for two
days, and I couldn't handle it... There was a new
kid there and he's like, "Oh, I heard about you.
You're that dirty little troublemaking atheist."[13]

Should Young Atheists Really Have to Pray to Play?

How could anyone hear that story and not get angry? This
wasn't just one Christian coach who had it out for Nicole. This
wasn't just the administrators at the school conspiring against
one of their own students. This was the *whole community* trying
to run an atheist and her family out of town.

Nicole dealt with a level of bullying that no one—much
less a high school student—should ever have to endure. It would
have been a lot easier to keep quiet about her beliefs and just
recite a prayer that should have meant nothing to her, but Nicole
chose the more courageous route. She wasn't ashamed of being
an atheist and she didn't want to hide that part of her identity
from her classmates. She suffered the consequences because of
it.

Katherine Stewart, author of the 2012 book *The Good
News Club: The Christian Right's Stealth Assault on America's
Children*, reiterated how difficult it must have been for Nicole to
stand up for her unpopular religious views:

... few fifteen-year-olds have the courage to stand
alone, outside the prayer circle, with the entire
community watching, in defense of their
principles... For every Nicole, there are perhaps
thousands who quietly join the circle and mumble
the words. Many students praying at their sporting
endeavors are themselves nontheists or members
of other religious traditions. But they know that
the locker room is no place for dissent, and that a
refusal to participate could easily be construed as

a sign of lack of commitment to the team. They have learned that they have to pray to play.[14]

Maybe you're thinking this was just an isolated incident. It's Oklahoma. It's the Bible Belt. It's a small, rural school district. It happened *years* ago. It's awful, but surely it's not commonplace.

If you thought that, you'd be mistaken.

It turns out that a similar story took place more recently on the other side of the country involving a student named Jessica Ahlquist, another young female atheist whose outspokenness made her the victim of harassment from both teenagers and adults.

Jessica Ahlquist's Story

Jessica's story actually begins several decades before she was even born. In 1963, the first-ever graduating class from Cranston High School West, a large public school in Rhode Island, gifted the school with two murals that would be painted on opposite walls of the new auditorium. On the left side of the auditorium would be the mural featuring the school creed. On the right side would be an eight-foot-tall, four-foot-wide "banner" stating the school prayer:

Our Heavenly Father.

Grant us each day the desire to do our best.
To grow mentally and morally as well as physically.
To be kind and helpful to our classmates and teachers.
To be honest with ourselves as well as with others.
Help us to be good sports and smile when we lose as well as when we win.
Teach us the value of true friendship.

Help us always to conduct ourselves so as to bring
credit to Cranston High School West.

Amen.

David Bradley, a member of the student council at the
time, wrote the prayer and he believed, even a half-century later,
that it was "part of the fabric of Cranston High School West."
Bradley felt that, because his prayer was non-denominational, it
would offend no one.[15]

For a while, it looked like Bradley was right. Only one
person had ever publicly complained about the prayer—but the
matter was quietly "resolved" without the banner being taken
down (or painted over).[16] In 2010, nearly fifty years after the
prayer mural went up, it was hit with a second, much more
serious, challenge. This time, a parent in the district contacted
the ACLU of Rhode Island for help. The reason was
straightforward: The banner promoted religion with its first and
last lines, so it was deemed unconstitutional.[17] The ACLU agreed:
It had to come down. They informed the school board about the
concern.

When the school board held its next meeting, the
members voted to do a little more research on the matter before
making a final decision. The last thing they wanted to do was
risk losing a costly legal battle.

Jessica Ahlquist was a sophomore at Cranston in the fall
of 2010 and she thought the decision should be fairly obvious. *Of
course the banner had to come down. Why was there even a
debate about it?* Her friend had told her about the banner at the
end of her freshman year and Jessica created a Facebook group
called "Help us remove that prayer from Cranston West High
School" (*sic*) to gather support for her side.

When the school board subcommittee finally met that
November to talk about the issue, Jessica attended the meeting
and spoke to them (as well as a handful of local residents also in
the crowd) about why the banner needed to go. She also shared
a piece of information with them that no one outside her family

had ever heard before: She was an atheist. As soon as she uttered the "A" word, there was an audible gasp from the crowd. Whispers permeated the room. When Jessica sat down after her speech, she heard an audience member mumble, "that little witch."[18]

At the time, there were fewer than twenty people in her Facebook group.

On March 7, 2011, after months of deliberation, the school board chose to ignore Jessica's plea and the ACLU's advice. They voted 4-3 in favor of keeping the banner in place. That decision started a chain reaction. Immediately, the ACLU vowed to file a lawsuit against the district. The board responded by taking up a voluntary collection in defense of the banner and searching for legal partners who would represent them free of charge.[19] (Eventually, the Becket Fund for Religious Liberty took the case on their behalf.[20])

In order for the ACLU's lawsuit to proceed, they needed someone from the school willing to represent their side in the case. Jessica was an obvious choice. With her parents' approval, Jessica signed on as the ACLU's lead plaintiff. She said that, as an atheist, she felt "excluded, ostracized and devalued" by the school because she didn't agree with the prayer. Furthermore, it was unconstitutional—a government endorsement of religion—and she objected to the school breaking the law.[21] The lawsuit also stated that Ahlquist had suffered "stress and anxiety, feelings of exclusion and isolation within her community, and fear of physical harm and retaliation" for her opposition to the banner.

The morning after the federal lawsuit was filed, Jessica overheard her classmates talking about how she was "mad retarded" for trying to challenge the banner. They weren't any kinder to her face, calling her a "media whore," a "stupid atheist," and a tool of the ACLU.[22] When the Pledge of Allegiance was recited in her homeroom that morning, students looked in her direction as they yelled the words "under God."

At one point later that month, the Mayor of Cranston, Allan Fung, visited the school to speak about his life as a Chinese-

American. The event was held in the auditorium, and Fung was asked for his opinion on the prayer banner. As he pointed to it with an outstretched hand, he proudly proclaimed, "I would like to see that prayer stay exactly where it is!" Jessica was in the room at the time and remained seated while the rest of her classmates stood up and applauded. What was supposed to be an uplifting talk turned into yet another opportunity to pick on the girl wearing the Scarlet "A."

Over the course of the next several months, Jessica's Facebook group grew to several hundred members. While most were very supportive, some commenters made Jessica's problems worse. One of them suggested urinating on the banner, a statement Jessica quickly disavowed. Unfortunately, word spread that Jessica herself had made the remark. Not wanting someone else's statement to haunt her, she shut down that group and began a new one: "Support the Removal of the Cranston High School West Prayer."[23] The membership for the new group grew even faster than the last one, well into the thousands. All of this occurred while the banner's future was still undecided.

On January 11, 2012, ten months after the lawsuit had been filed, U.S. District Court Judge Ronald R. Lagueux issued his ruling: The prayer banner *was* unconstitutional and the school district had ten days to take it down. Jessica and the ACLU had won the case.[24]

I had been following this case ever since the school board was considering what to do about the prayer, and Jessica's demeanor during the whole ordeal amazed me. I felt she deserved to be rewarded for the courage she had shown throughout the previous year, so I set up a scholarship fund for her on my website. That post sat in "draft" mode for months as I waited for the judge to announce his decision. When his ruling came down, my fundraiser went up.

There was no time to celebrate the decision, though; Jessica was still caught in the crossfire of religious extremists who believed their rights had somehow been stripped away. For several days, there was a mixture of good news and bad news as the school board wondered whether or not it should appeal the ruling.

Jessica was subjected to a variety of threats from all directions. On Twitter and Facebook, people condemned her to hell, threatened to jump her and punch her in school, and made jokes about raping her. Someone posted her home address on a public forum.[25] She stayed home for several days after the ruling.[26] The one bright spot amid all this chaos was that Jessica had an army of atheists on her side who were quick to take screenshots of these comments and send them to local authorities so that they could take action on them—and they did. Police were summoned to keep an eye on both the high school and Jessica's house, and the students who had made the threats were brought in for questioning.[27]

Local politicians also lashed out against her. State Representative Peter Palumbo appeared on a morning radio show and called Jessica "an evil little thing" on air.[28] State Senator Beth Moura took to Twitter and snidely called Jessica the "ACLU sweetheart."[29] In retaliation to Palumbo's comment, JT Eberhard, with the support of bloggers at FreethoughtBlogs.com, created shirts with the phrase "Evil Little Thing" and began selling them to Jessica's supporters.[30] All the profits from sales—more than $8,000 in total—were then donated to Jessica's scholarship fund.

When the Freedom From Religion Foundation wanted to congratulate Jessica on her victory, they contacted a few different florists near Cranston to deliver flowers to her. Four different companies *refused to fulfill the order*. However, an out-of-state company, Glimpse of Gaia, stepped in and delivered flowers to Jessica's doorstep. They even included a second bouquet (at no cost) with the message, "Glimpse of Gaia fully supports our First Amendment and will not be bullied by those who do not. Here's to you, Jessica Ahlquist."[31] During "Florist-gate," there was another surge of donations to Jessica's scholarship.

In fact, for several weeks, my inbox was flooded with donation receipts from PayPal. They came in amounts ranging from one dollar to hundreds of dollars. By the time the fundraising drive had ended on my site, 1,793 individuals had contributed over $48,000 to a scholarship in Jessica's honor. Combined with sales from the "Evil Little Thing" T-shirts and contributions sent directly to the American Humanist Association (which handled all the money), donors raised a grand total of $62,618. All of that money will be made available to Jessica to cover items like tuition and books when she heads to college.

Just over a month after Judge Lagueux's ruling, the Cranston School Committee voted 5-2 in favor of *not* appealing his decision. Instead of pursuing further legal challenges—that it would likely lose—the committee decided to cut its losses. The district and the city of Cranston agreed to split down the middle the $150,000 in legal fees they owed the ACLU.

Cranston High School West has since permanently painted over the wall where the banner used to be displayed.

The Aftermath for the Young Women

It's hard to hear about what young women like Nicole and Jessica went through because they stood up for their non-religious beliefs and their Constitutional rights. Their courage is inspiring and I hope others follow in their footsteps.

Yet, despite all the similarities in their stories, their outcomes couldn't have been more different.

Nicole Smalkowski was forced to leave her school. She had relatively little support from the atheist community at large during her short-lived public high school career, and most atheists would probably still be unaware of what happened in Hardesty if not for a brief segment about her story that aired on ABC's *20/20*. Her battle appeared to be a solitary one, and after her case ended, the atheist spotlight turned off as well. It wasn't until I began researching this book that I realized how much had happened in Nicole's life since her days at Hardesty High School.

Jessica Ahlquist, on the other hand, received an outpouring of support from the atheist community and it helped sustain her throughout the ordeal. (The donations didn't hurt, either.) Atheists had driven in from other states just to defend her at school board meetings. Jessica's battle also captured national headlines, with glowing profiles of her appearing in the *New York Times,*[32] National Public Radio,[33] and ABC World News.[34]

Both young women stood up for their atheism and dealt with social ostracism and threats as a result. But only one had a positive outcome. Why was that? Was it where they lived? Was it the nature of their cases? Was it the type of media coverage their stories received?

Sure, all of those things may have been factors, but I would argue that there's one reason that towers above the rest: The difference was *almost entirely due* to the rise of a support system for young atheists that has only recently blossomed. Jessica Ahlquist is only one of the many beneficiaries of a revolution in the way Secular Americans support young atheists in this country—and that revolution wasn't quite ready to help Nicole Smalkowski in 2004.

This book is about that revolution and what all of us can do to help the cause.

As a high school teacher for the past six years, I've seen firsthand how tough it can be to be a student who dares to be different. It's hardly surprising to say that, in much of the country, declaring yourself to be an atheist is akin to painting a target on your back. Additionally, as an atheist blogger, I'm constantly inundated with stories about young atheists who inspire me to be a better activist and mentor, as well as stories about school districts where promoting Christianity seems to be a part of the curriculum.

When I hear about Nicole and Jessica and countless other students like them who are atheists and suffer consequences because of it, it affects me personally because I know I probably have students in my classroom who are just like them. I don't want any of my students to feel bad or get bullied because they took an unpopular stand on religion. Even though my job requires me to be a teacher first and an atheist second, I don't have to stand on the sidelines when these incidents occur.

The number of non-religious teenagers is growing like never before, a topic we'll explore in more detail in the next chapter. Nicole and Jessica aren't the only students dealing with problems because of their atheism, and I suspect we'll hear many more stories like theirs in the coming years as atheism becomes more of a potent force in our society. More atheists will be ostracized, more administrators will try to prevent non-religious students from forming groups, and more religious politicians and organizations will try to push their beliefs onto students in retaliation. Atheists may not always be physically beaten up as many young LGBT students have been, but the social pressure to keep their atheism hidden is very real.

At the same time, over the past decade, the number of non-religious people, especially in younger demographics, has increased dramatically.

The number of secular student groups at high schools and colleges has grown more than tenfold, thanks to the support of national umbrella organizations like the Secular Student Alliance and Center For Inquiry On Campus.[35] The number of forums, blogs, books, and podcasts dedicated to the topic of atheism has skyrocketed. That means there are more ways to let young atheists know they're not alone, more conversations about religious doubt taking place at the high school and college levels, and more students learning how to fight back against the illegal religious whims of their teachers and administrators.

This book will cover all of that. It will also talk about what those of us who graduated from high school a long time ago can do to help students who are just now realizing they don't believe in a god.

Whether you're an atheist, an educator, an administrator, a parent, a researcher, or even a religious person just curious about what young atheists are up to, I hope this book helps educate you about young atheists and serves as a useful resource. The purpose of the book is not to point blame at specific religious people who are obstacles to atheists exercising their rights. The purpose of this book is to discuss the fact that those rights are attacked, period, and explore what we can do about it.

All students deserve the opportunity to explore their religious views openly and safely. But too many young atheists have not had that chance. We can put a stop to that by giving them the support they need while at the same time empowering young atheists to develop their identities. The first step is to understand the types of problems they face.

2

Taking Attendance

How Many Young Atheists Are There?

Before we talk more extensively about the obstacles young atheists have to deal with, it's important to answer a pretty basic question: *How many young atheists are there?*

The short answer is: We have no idea.

The long answer is: We have *some* idea... Considering how many studies there have been regarding Americans and their religious beliefs, we ought to have some grasp on the answer. But when it comes to studying young atheists, researchers have had to grapple with two big issues: How to define "young" and how broadly they can stretch the definition of "atheist."

Let's start with the word "young." For ethical reasons, research scientists cannot just "call up" minors and ask them about something as personal as their religious beliefs.[1] You would need to get parental permission first and, even then, it's hard to know if the responses you received would be honest (imagine if the parents were nearby when sensitive questions were asked...). Trying to go through the public schools—even with parental consent—would pose a host of additional problems, including the lack of uniformity of schools, making sure teachers administered the survey properly, and getting the students to take the survey seriously. Therefore, the only reliable data we have about what religious beliefs people hold involve those eighteen years of age or older. Thankfully, we can still learn a lot from that information.

The second problem is with the word "atheist." Because researchers are trying to extract meaningful information from mountains of data, they often group together people with similar belief systems. Consider this: When you want to know the religious beliefs of Americans, does it make more sense to separate Lutherans, Methodists, and Presbyterians, or is it more meaningful to simply combine them and say what percentage of Americans are simply "Christian"? Similarly, in the eyes of the researchers, it doesn't always make sense to distinguish between the various labels underneath the "atheist umbrella" (including agnostics, Humanists, Brights, naturalists, freethinkers, etc.), especially because each group is relatively insignificant on its own. So researchers tend to lump all of those groups into a category called "Unaffiliated" or "None." If we're lucky, they might break down that category into slightly smaller subgroups, but that doesn't always happen.

Sometimes, this lumping can go too far. For example, in addition to atheists, agnostics, and the like, the "Nones" may also include people who are "spiritual but not religious," Christians who say "I'm not Christian; I'm a follower of Jesus," people who attend church but don't consider themselves religious, and people who are currently in the process of seeking out a faith that's right for them but don't have a particular preference just yet. In other words, the "Nones" *may include people who believe in God*, or people who, at the very least, participate in some religious rituals.

All of these issues make it tougher for us to figure out what percentage of high school students (or teenagers in general) don't believe in God.

But, like I said, it's not an entirely impossible task. In fact, we know quite a bit about what young Americans think about religion. Patterns have emerged to the point that religious groups frequently express their concerns about them.

So what does the data show?

It shows us that the number of young atheists appears to be growing and that trend shows no sign of slowing down. Every study varies a bit, but we can look at many of them systematically in order to gather helpful information.

Let's start by looking at the "Millennial generation." This is the group of people aged 18-29 at the time of the survey and it is the youngest demographic we have reliable information about.

A Gallup poll from June 2011 asked Americans if they believed in God and grouped the responses by age range.[2]

94 percent of people 65 and older said they believed in God.

So did 94 percent of people 50-64.[3]

So did 94 percent of people 30-49.

But **when it came to the Millennials, the number dropped sharply, to 84 percent**. In other words, the youngest demographic was also the least likely to believe in God.

To delve a little deeper into these numbers, the American Religious Identification Survey (ARIS) is more helpful because it is arguably the most comprehensive survey of religion we have to work with.[4] Published roughly every ten years with the most recent report coming out in 2008, ARIS reported that **22 percent of the Millennial population professed no religious beliefs**.[5] Compared to the 15 percent of "Nones" ARIS found in the general population, this generation was less religious than the others. More importantly, of the Millennial Nones, fewer than a third of them said they identified as a None at the age of twelve, meaning that *most of them lost their faith somewhere along the path to adulthood.*[6]

A more recent survey (February 2010), by the Pew Forum on Religion & Public Life, found that the percentage of non-religious 18- to 29-year-olds had increased slightly.[7] According to them, **26 percent of Millennials were religiously unaffiliated**.[8]

That number went up even more a couple of years later. In October 2012, the Pew Research Center's Forum on Religion and Public Life released a report that was very blunt about the "rise of the nones"[9]:

> The number of Americans who do not identify with any religion continues to grow at a rapid pace...

A third of adults under 30 have no religious affiliation (32%), compared with just one-in-ten who are 65 and older (9%). And young adults today are much more likely to be unaffiliated than previous generations were at a similar stage in their lives.[10]

It seems safe to say the percentage of Millennials who are unaffiliated with religion is at least in the low-to-mid twenties, steadily rising, with no peak or plateau in sight. More importantly, it's higher than anything we see in older demographics.

Here's an alternative question: Are Millennials at least *questioning* their faith? That's what the Pew Research Center For The People and The Press wanted to know in June of 2012. They asked people if they agreed or disagreed with the following statement: "I never doubt the existence of God."[11] Devoutly religious people would likely agree with that statement, while hardcore atheists would disagree. Typically, the number of people agreeing with the statement has been high—between 85 and 90 percent—no matter what age group you look at. But a strange thing has been happening for Millennials. While all the other age groups fluctuate up and down only slightly, the Millennials show a steep decline in recent years. **In fact, while 83 percent of Millennials said they never doubted God's existence in 2007, that number had fallen to 68 percent by 2012.**[12]

That means young Americans are questioning their faith and finding more reasons to be skeptical about it. They may not all be atheists, but many may be heading down that path.

Can we extrapolate from here? Can we figure out what *teenagers* believe based on all this data? We can't answer that with certainty, but we have one advantage. Most studies, like the ones already mentioned, sort the responses by the age of the respondents. But some, instead of looking at the age group 18-29, look to the ages 18-24 or 18-25. Because it's a slightly younger group, with a lower average age, it offers a bit more insight into the demographic we're most eager to learn about. (The most ideal survey for our purposes would tell us what *only* eighteen-year-olds think, but that information has not yet been made available.)

We have two surveys that shed insight into this subset of the Millennials. One, from the Public Religion Research Institute[13], reported in 2012 that **25 percent of the 18-24-year-old population was "Unaffiliated."**[14] No big change there from what we saw before.

Another study, by the Pew Research Center For The People and The Press, looked at "Generation Next," ages 18-25.[15] But instead of lumping together the entire "Unaffiliated" crowd like most of the other surveys, they used a category called "No religion/Atheist/Agnostic." What they found was astonishing. In the late 1980s, only 11 percent of Generation Next had put themselves in this category. But **by 2006, the percentage of Nexters citing "No religion" had nearly doubled to 20 percent**.[16] And they didn't even include those Nexters who were "religious and unaffiliated."

Survey after survey show a rise in the number of both non-religious and religiously-unaffiliated Americans. Atheists know this. Religious groups know this. Researchers know this. Even if they're not happy with the results, there's no disputing the trends.

Why Does All of This Matter?

This matters because there are many young atheists who believe they are alone in their thoughts. They don't talk openly about their lack of religious beliefs because they think (often with good reason) everybody they know will ostracize them. They don't want to be the "village atheist" at a time when approval from their peers is so vital to their well-being. They don't form communities to discuss and debate these ideas because they don't believe their peers are interested.

But they're not alone. We can safely say that *at least* one out of every five students strongly questions or doubts the existence of God. That's what these surveys tell us. In fact, there may be *many* non-theistic students at their schools; they just have to be able to find each other. If we can find a way to bring them together, support them, and give them the tools they need to—forgive my phrasing—take a deeper walk with their atheism, we can empower them to spread reason to their classmates as well as future generations. No doubt many of them would take advantage of that opportunity.

I became an atheist at the age of fourteen. At the time, I could count the number of other non-religious people I knew on one hand, and that made the transition to atheism really tough for me. I had to go through the paradigm shift one takes when adopting one belief system for another in virtual isolation. But if I had just asked around or, better yet, had some sort of forum in which to discuss these newly-forming thoughts in my mind, I probably would have realized atheists were all around me, even in high school. There was no reason to think I was alone.

What the Research Won't Tell You

Two final points about all these results: First, I suspect that all of these numbers are underestimating the true non-religious population. There is still a stigma associated with not believing in God and, even in anonymous surveys, people may not want to admit their atheism. It's also possible that people who are culturally religious but don't actually believe in a higher power still label themselves as religious. What would the numbers look like if everyone labeled themselves accurately? We don't know for sure, but I suspect it's significantly higher than we're seeing now.

Additionally, I've ignored the question of *why* young people are non-religious in the first place. That's an intentional move on my part. There are so many reasons that it would take another book to discuss them—and, indeed, many have been written on the subject. But I can offer a few basic reasons I've come across in my conversations with other atheists:

1) Some of them were never raised religious to begin with.

2) Some left the faith of their parents after they began questioning it and found that the evidence pointed away from what their religious leaders proclaimed to be true. (That's what happened to me.)

3) Some found church members and leaders to be hypocritical, or against equal rights for the LGBT community, or too controlling, or opposed to giving women the same opportunities afforded to men, or too political, and they wanted to get out.

David Niose, the author of *Nonbeliever Nation: The Rise of Secular Americans*, believes the most vocal atheists may come from the most religious homes and communities:

> Often students point to the pervasive influence of conservative religion in their lives, which might explain why some of the strongest student groups can be found in areas known for religious conservatism. Just as reformed smokers are the strongest anti-smoking advocates, young people coming from fundamentalist families—having grown up with images of fire and brimstone, fear of damnation, and constant references to the Bible, God, Satan, good and evil—are often the most enthusiastic about their identity as secular individuals.[17]

For our purposes, though, the reasons young Americans become atheists are irrelevant. We're interested in what they face now that they *are* atheists. While obstacles are found just about everywhere, the bulk of the battles seem to take place inside the schools these students attend, and the people who ought to have the students' best interests at heart turn out to be their biggest foes. So let's begin by looking at how administrators have blocked or impeded the formation of student groups for atheists.

3

The Principal's Office

When Administrators Attack

In 1977, administrators at the University of Missouri at Kansas City told a group of Christian students that they could no longer hold regular meetings on campus.[1] That news came as a surprise to the Christians since their group, Cornerstone, was a registered student organization at the school and such groups were *always* given free meeting space. Without that, where else were they going to pray, sing, and hold Bible studies? Where else could they squeeze in the 125 students who attended their meetings?

The school's rationale was that Cornerstone was a *religious* group and the university prohibited giving space to groups for "religious worship or religious teaching." The students were essentially given two options: Meet in a campus chapel or meet secretly. Neither was a viable choice for them. The nearest campus chapel was 125 miles away at the University of Missouri at Columbia. Building one at UMKC would cost several hundred thousand dollars, money the students would have to raise themselves.[2] And the students never seriously considered meeting in secret—why couldn't they discuss and practice their faith publicly?

Eleven of the Cornerstone members soon filed a lawsuit against the school, saying that the university had discriminated against them because of their religious beliefs. The case eventually made it to the Supreme Court. In *Widmar v Vincent* (1981), the justices ruled 8-1 in favor of the students, saying that because the university already recognized over one hundred student groups, all of which had access to the school's facilities, the school had to give access to religious student groups as well.

In what would later be seen as a cruel twist, the Court said that its ruling only applied to *university* students because they were "less impressionable than younger students." So the question of whether the law applied to religious organizations at public high schools still lingered.

In the early 1980s, around the time the Religious Right was beginning to gather strength, Christian leaders knew they wanted to establish student groups at public high schools. It was a way to save souls and secure soldiers for future legal battles. The Supreme Court had put a stop to both school-sponsored prayers and mandatory Bible readings decades earlier, but it had not yet ruled against voluntary after-school Bible clubs.

In an effort to make sure Christian groups *could* form at the high school level, Senator Mark Hatfield, a Republican from Oregon and a devout Baptist, introduced legislation that came to be known as the Equal Access Act of 1984. The Equal Access Act said that any public high school that received government funding and already had at least one non-curricular club that met outside of class time (like Yoga Club or Drama Club) could not ban student groups on the basis of religion.[3]

The Act passed in the House 337-77 and in the Senate 88-11.[4] President Ronald Reagan signed it into law on August 11, 1984. In a nutshell, the Act applied the ruling in *Widmar* to secondary schools.

At the time, televangelist Pat Robertson called it a "major landmark decision and a tremendous victory."[5] The late Jerry Falwell was also ecstatic, boasting, "We knew we couldn't win on school prayer [in Congress], but 'equal access' gets us what we wanted all along."[6]

What Falwell may not have realized was that atheists would also become beneficiaries of the legislation. The Equal Access Act banned discrimination not just on the basis of religion, but also political and philosophical viewpoints. As it stood, any high school that had a Chess Club could also have an Atheist Club. The same law that let the Fellowship of Christian

Athletes meet after school has since given rise to the Gay-Straight Alliance. (The ghost of Jerry Falwell must be thrilled.)

In 2011, Secretary of Education Arne Duncan reiterated what the Equal Access Act allowed and when it could be applied.[7] As long as it was a public school receiving federal funding and allowing at least one non-curricular group to meet on campus outside of class time, he said, the EAA would be in effect.

Duncan continued by emphasizing that those schools had to allow students to form a group, even around an unpopular idea.

Those schools had to offer students the same access to publicity that all other groups had, like posting flyers around the school or having the club's meeting times read during morning announcements.

If there were already student groups affiliated with a national organization (like Key Club or the National Honor Society), then other groups were allowed to affiliate with national organizations as well—like the Secular Student Alliance, a national umbrella group for non-religious students. (In other words, no group would have to change its name just because the subject matter at hand was objectionable.)

What about faculty sponsors? Did a high school group need to find a staff member who supported its message in order to meet? Nope. And, once again, we have Christians to thank.

In 1985, after the Equal Access Act had been signed into law, senior Bridget Mergens wanted to start a Bible club at Westside High School in Omaha, Nebraska. When she approached her principal with the idea, he rejected it. His concern was that allowing a pro-Christian group to meet at school would be a violation of church/state separation, not a logical consequence of it, as many administrators now believe. Specifically, he told her that her group could not have a faculty sponsor because that would be seen as an endorsement of Christianity, and without a faculty sponsor there could be no group.

Mergens wasn't buying it. With the help of Christian lawyers, her case went through the legal system, all the way up to the Supreme Court.[8] *Westside School District v. Mergens* (1990) resulted in another 8-1 decision, in which the Court agreed that the school could not stop Mergens' group from forming. Just because a school had a Christian club didn't mean the school endorsed Christianity. Just because a Christian club had a faculty sponsor didn't mean that sponsor necessarily believed in or was promoting Christianity. In fact, the Court even alluded to the ability of teenagers to understand that, something it was reluctant to do back in 1981:

> We think that secondary school students are mature enough and are likely to understand that a school does not endorse or support student speech that it merely permits on a nondiscriminatory basis.[9]

How does that decision apply to atheists today? It's very easy to tell atheist college students where to find faculty sponsors for their groups—just look to your science or philosophy departments because the odds are pretty good you'll find a non-religious professor willing to attend and participate in group meetings, or at least sign off on the paperwork. At the high school level, though, finding an atheist teacher isn't as simple. *But it doesn't matter.* The school has an obligation to let the atheists meet. Even if the students can't find a teacher who supports their mission, they have every right to be a registered club at the school, even if it means having a faculty member assigned to them for the purpose of supervision. And if no sponsor can be found, another adult—a parent, perhaps—could step in. Or the sponsor requirement could be waived altogether.

To stop a group from meeting because they couldn't find a like-minded sponsor would be a violation of the Equal Access Act.

And yet, this chapter is all about administrators who try to stop atheist clubs from forming. How can they get away with it when the law seems to prevent exactly that problem?

The simplest way is to just ignore the law, ban the atheist club, and hope the students don't know any better.

Another way—one that is theoretically allowed within the law—would be to ban *all* non-curricular groups entirely. But that extreme approach would probably stop some popular clubs from meeting, an outcome that would likely lead to a lot of angry phone calls from parents. Plus, the U.S. Department of Education has already warned against that measure, saying that "successfully closing a previously open forum will often prove difficult" because courts will be on the lookout to make sure all clubs remaining are "genuinely curricular." In short: Don't even think about it.

If secular students are armed with a basic understanding of the Equal Access Act, they have an almost-foolproof way to counter principals and faculty members who try to dissuade them from forming atheist groups. In fact, as you're about to see, many courageous young atheists have forced their school officials to backtrack and change their ways because they knew they were on the right side of the law.

It's a good thing, too. Having these groups for atheists can be the difference between being accepted and feeling isolated, between having a safe venue to discuss your religious doubts and having to keep them suppressed. In schools where being an atheist automatically puts you at a disadvantage, it is vital to have a community of like-minded students who can prove the stigmas wrong and educate the student body on why atheists, too, can be good, kind, moral people.

In fact, Leondré, a high school student from Florida whom I spoke with, started his atheist group precisely because he wanted to show other students that there was nothing wrong with people who didn't believe in God:

> I felt the strong need for representation of the atheist body within our school. Each individual

might be picked on by friends or parents or society at large, but it's good to have reassurance that you're *not* a terrible person, *not* immoral, *not* crazy because you think differently than the mainstream.[10]

Even those who are unsure where these students get their morality from can hopefully get behind their right to form a group. And while the Equal Access Act seems like a fairly straightforward law, school administrators have shown time and time again that they often don't understand its basics. When high school students have tried to form atheist groups, they've faced unfair (and in many cases illegal) resistance from school officials. It doesn't just happen in rural America and the Bible Belt. It happens all over the country. What we find is that when one or two school officials don't want to see an atheist group form, they will do whatever they need to do—leveraging all the power their titles bestow upon them, if necessary—to scare the students into backing down. They do this, presumably, despite knowing that the law was designed to put a stop to these very practices.

What kinds of obstacles do these school officials present to atheist group leaders?

When Savannah Lanz wanted to start the Freethinkers Society at Johnsburg High School in Illinois in 2009, she was told she couldn't advertise group meetings by putting up flyers in the building, something all the other student groups were able to do.[11]

When a high school junior in Oklahoma wanted to begin a Secular Student Alliance affiliate in 2010, his principal pulled him out of class and said: "I have information that you are trying to start a school-led *hate group*." The student explained that his group was anything but hateful, and the principal seemed to let up, but that wasn't the end of the issue. The faculty member who was lined up to sponsor the group said she could no longer support it because "she was told it would be a very bad career move." Even though the group could legally continue without her, the other students lost their interest and the group faded away before it ever officially began.[12]

A similar story occurred at Melbourne High School in Florida, where secular students wanted to begin a Fellowship of Atheist and Agnostic Athletes (an alternative to the ever-present Fellowship of Christian Athletes). Founder Jade Sigler had a faculty sponsor ready to go as well as a petition in support of the group signed by fifty-six interested students. But not only was the group rejected by the school's administration for being "too controversial,"[13] the potential faculty sponsor was given "a friendly reminder that pursuing the club could be bad as a new teacher."[14] This was, in other words, a subtle threat that the teacher's job could be in jeopardy for becoming an atheist group's sponsor.

Even junior high school teachers can face the same pressure from above. Duncan Henderson wanted to start a freethinking group at Auburn Junior High School in Alabama, but after his potential faculty sponsor spoke with the school's principal, she told Duncan's father that she was "very uncomfortable" about taking on that role. So Duncan's dad spoke directly to the principal, who told him "I don't think you'll find a sponsor for this club on this campus."[15]

In some cases, the principals don't stop the atheist clubs from meeting, but do whatever they can to hide the dreaded "A" word from the eyes of the students. In 2012, the Secular Student Alliance at La Porte High School in Texas advertised their group with a sign reading: "ATHEIST: It's not a bad word! It is someone who either believes there is no god (or gods) or has a lack of belief in a god (or gods)." There was also a picture of the American flag on the middle of the sign and details about upcoming meetings at the bottom. When Michael, the group leader, gave a copy of the flyer to the principal for approval (as is customary), what he got back later surprised him. The principal had crossed out the entire definition of an atheist—with multiple X's—adding this explanatory note: "Will not allow this because it could disrupt the education process at LPHS."[16] Apparently, the word "Atheist" was too offensive for students' eyes. (Are dictionaries banned from the school, too?)

Stephanie, a student from Missouri, discovered a similar double standard when it came to putting up posters in her school. When her group wanted to participate in National Ask An Atheist Day, she noticed a poster for the aforementioned Fellowship of Christian Athletes. It read: "Mornings are rough... Have a free breakfast and learn about Jesus! Thursdays, 7:00 A.M." Alongside it were the group's name and the room number. So Stephanie made her posters along the same lines. Some simply said, "Ask An Atheist Day! Thursday, April 19." Other signs pointed out that group members would be wearing special shirts indicating that they could answer other students' questions. A couple of hours after the posters went up, Stephanie was pulled out of class because a faculty member found her posters to be "offensive" and "anti-Christian" and wanted them taken down. It took several emails between JT Eberhard (at the time, the high school specialist at the Secular Student Alliance) and the principal before her posters were allowed to go back up.

In all of those cases, the students were essentially helpless against the wishes of their administrators. But they didn't have to be. When students are aware that groups like the Secular Student Alliance and the Freedom From Religion Foundation specialize in dealing with these issues—as Stephanie did—the controversies usually come to an abrupt end. All it takes is an email informing the national atheist groups what's happening in your school and their staffs will handle it from there.

Alexa, a high school student from North Carolina, knew that. She wanted to form a Secular Student Alliance at her school and even found a willing faculty sponsor (one who, interestingly enough, believed in God). Her fellow officers drafted a Constitution for the group—the first step to getting official recognition—and submitted it to the principal for approval. After weeks of not hearing back, Alexa scheduled an in-person meeting with him. When she arrived for the meeting, she was told the principal was out of the building. So she tried again.

When they finally met, it was clear to her that he had not even looked at their Constitution. By the end of the meeting, Alexa was no closer to having her group approved. That's when she contacted JT Eberhard at the Secular Student Alliance. He sent the principal an email explaining the legal problems with denying her group approval. Within a couple of days, Alexa found out her group was approved. "I'm guessing the email put 'the fear of God' in that poor man," she later joked.[17]

Adam Butler's problems arose before the Secular Student Alliance came into existence, but he was fortunately aware of the other resources at his disposal. Butler was a senior at Pelham High School in Alabama in 1996 when he saw signs advertising a student-led Christian group called First PrioriTy. (The T was in the shape of a cross.) They met each week before school and Adam wondered whether he could start the Pelham Freethinker Association in response. He wrote an editorial for his school newspaper, only to be told it was cut due to "size constraints." So he printed out the article, made six hundred copies, and passed it out to students in the lunchroom and gym lobby. That's when the principal stepped in. He told Adam and his friend that they couldn't hand out literature like that without approval. So Adam asked him directly about the formation of the club. The principal's response was an immediate refusal: "I can assure you: there will be no 'Freethinker's Club' at PHS."[18] Adam pressed on, though, and the principal told him he would think about it.

Week after week, Adam went back to the principal's office to see if his club was given a green light. Week after week, the principal told him "No." This went on for three months. It dawned on Adam that his graduation wasn't far away, so maybe the school was just trying to push the decision back to a point when he would no longer be attending school. But he was intent on getting his group started before he graduated.

That's when Adam called up the Alabama state affiliate of the Freedom From Religion Foundation. Chapter President Pat Cleveland gave him some advice: Document the principal's replies. So instead of walking into his office each week, Adam began sending the principal emails. The response was still a resounding, "No." Armed with the email proof, which Adam sent along to Cleveland, the principal and superintendent began getting phone calls from the FFRF and ACLU (which had also been contacted by Cleveland), letting them know that what they were doing was in violation of the Equal Access Act.

On April 8, 1996, the principal at Pelham High School told Adam he could begin the Pelham Freethinker Association.[19] It was a month before he received his diploma. Adam knew it was the pressure from those outside groups that helped his administration finally see the light:

> In my opinion, [Principal Tom] Ferguson did not want to be the first Shelby County principal to be sued for religious bigotry. I didn't expect it to last long... and it didn't. I came to see him in the office and he told me that he was trying to look past his own private beliefs, and the group was allowed to meet.[20]

There was only one condition, the principal said. Adam had to tell the Alabama Freethought Association (Cleveland's group) and FFRF to stop calling the school's main office.[21] Adam politely obliged.

While the group had a solid one-month run, it didn't make it to the next school year. The parents of the student Adam believed would take his place as the group's president told him he couldn't be a part of the club. No one else wanted to become, as Adam put it, "the poster child for a group that had spawned so much controversy."[22]

Micah White's battle with his administration was even tougher. White was a junior at Grand Blanc High School in Michigan in 1999. Every time the subject of an atheist club was brought up, his administrators gave him a run-around. The principal told Micah he needed a faculty sponsor and the approval of the vice-principal. The vice-principal, Bill Chittle, said Micah's group could meet, but they couldn't announce group meetings over the public address system or put up signs to advertise (both of which were allowed for other clubs). Micah knew this was illegal and gently objected. Chittle retorted: "Stop worrying so much about the law and worry about what Grand Blanc High School allows." (Months later, the principal admitted that American law did, in fact, apply to the Michigan school.)

Eventually, Micah was told he could start his group. But only if he renamed it from the "Atheist Club" to the "Alternative Religions Club."

That's when Micah took the journal he had used to document his interactions with the school and sent it to the local ACLU and Americans United for Separation of Church and State. Immediately, both groups sent letters to the school threatening a lawsuit if such restrictions were applied. The principal, knowing he was on the losing end of any potential lawsuit, caved and told Micah he could form his "Atheist Club," name intact.[23]

It Shouldn't Be This Hard

Why is there all this hassle just because some students want to be open about their atheism? Why can't administrators just allow atheist groups to form? It could be simple ignorance of the laws. It could be a visceral reaction to the idea of "atheist groups" in the first place. It could also be active discrimination, trying to prevent atheists from meeting on campus before they encourage other students to lose faith in God.

None of it is legal, though.

While filing a lawsuit may be warranted in some of these cases, it's not always the best course of action for the students involved. Few students dream of being a plaintiff in a court case; they don't want to draw unwanted attention from their classmates and teachers. They would much rather just have their group approved so they can hold meetings and have discussions about issues pertaining to atheism. It's also possible that they, like many of the administrators, don't know or don't understand what the law says. For all the lawsuits (or simply complaints) we hear about, there may be many more that go unfiled because the students just didn't know fighting back was an option.

For what it's worth, it wasn't right when Christians had to fight for their right to meet on campuses, either. If any religious group today faced the same struggle when forming a campus group, I have no doubt they would have atheists on their side, fighting for their rights even if the atheists disagreed with the religion in question. In the cases mentioned in this chapter, though, the atheists were more or less on their own. I wish I could tell you stories of how Christian students came to the defense of the atheist students as they encountered all these impediments, but those stories were either kept well under the radar or they never happened at all.

Before moving on, it's important to give credit to all the administrators who do the right thing and give these atheist groups their full support. Indeed, there are many principals out there who know the law and want to give atheist students the same opportunities as the religious ones. When I asked one principal if he had ever experienced any problems with atheist groups during his career, he was taken aback by the question itself, telling me, "The challenge [I encounter] is usually *over-access* by religious groups, not *equal access* by atheist groups."

If only asking for equal access was that simple a task for all students.

Since there are plenty of stories highlighting what can go wrong when starting a club, I want to end this chapter with a story of an administrator doing the right thing. Trevor Lynn, a student at Eureka High School in California, had no problems whatsoever beginning his group and said as much to a reporter in the summer of 2012:

> "The administration of our school really prides itself on being able to have a club for everybody," Lynn said. "They saw no reason to stop us."

> Now, his group—about seven members—meets to discuss philosophy and ethics and stage special events. In

September, the club will host joint lectures on evolution and creationism by a prominent freethought author and a local pastor.

"I think it is important, especially in high school where people are coming into their own beliefs, that we have a space where people can feel kind of secure in their nonbelief and have a meeting where they know there are other people like them," Lynn said. "That is the big reason I started the club."[24]

How would the other teenagers mentioned in this chapter have fared if they had Trevor's experience? How much better would their high school careers have been? And what are we doing to ensure equality for student groups everywhere?

There is no reason that an atheist group can't exist at just about every public high school in this country. But we need brave students who are willing to take the lead. The law is on their side and good administrators know that.

Unfortunately, administrators are only one of the obstacles to beginning atheist groups. It's tempting to believe that if we only educate them about the law, our problems will be solved. But that's wishful thinking. The opposition to atheist groups—and atheism in general—often comes from people who play a far more central role in students' lives. That resistance can be much more difficult to deal with, forcing many students to restrain their irreligious identities because they don't feel comfortable coming clean about their doubts.

4

Peer Pressure

Dealing with Friends and Family Members

A few years ago, Emily, a Sunday School teacher from Arkansas, handed me a set of drawings. Before giving them to me, she set up the situation: A church leader told Emily to have her fifth and sixth grade students draw what a Christian *looked* like on a blank outline of a gingerbread man.

Emily wasn't so sure that was a good idea.

To make matters worse, that was only half of the assignment. After the kids had drawn what a Christian looked like, they had to draw another picture... of what a *non-Christian* looked like.

Emily had no control over the curriculum, but she stressed to her students that there was no way to know whether or not people were Christians just by looking at them. You had to *talk* to them, hear their stories, get to know them. Looks were deceiving and this assignment was just playing into the stereotypes. But she did as she was told and handed the gingerbread men outlines to her students.

She had saved one of the student's drawings because it played into every fear she had when teaching the lesson. I braced myself. Emily must have noticed, too, because she nodded in agreement. We both knew where this was going.

This was the student's drawing of a "Christian":

There was a cross in his left hand. Neatly parted hair. Freckles. A speech bubble with the words "I LOVE GOD!!" inside of it. A banana in his right hand, perhaps symbolic of health, or an homage to an infamous video by evangelist Ray Comfort in which he calls a banana the "atheist's worst nightmare" because its yellow color, curvature toward your mouth, and easy-to-open tab at the top are all supposedly proof of God's existence. His clothes were nicely colored in with no white space left to fill.

Then I saw the same student's drawing of someone who *didn't* have Christ in his life:

In his right hand the infidel held a bottle, presumably filled with alcohol. Piercings went up and down both ears. A cigarette rested in his mouth. The sleeves on his shirt were ripped off (in anger?). The clothing remaining on his body was hastily colored in—the child had no inclination to color in the white spaces. A chain link tattoo had been drawn on his left arm while an anchor tattoo was on his right bicep; both were sticking out of his skin. His hair was a mess, unkempt, flying in all directions.

I think I was most offended by the unibrow.

What Happens As These Children Grow Up?

Are those drawings indicative of a bigger problem? I believe they are. I really don't think this child's parents were explicitly teaching him these "differences" at home (though they may have suggested it in subtler, possibly even subconscious ways). I don't think his pastor was teaching the congregation the universal characteristics of all atheists, either. Certainly, Emily wasn't responsible for it. But this kid picked it up from somewhere. More importantly, if his prejudice isn't corrected, those stereotypes are going to stay with him through high school, college, and maybe even beyond. This notion that "Christians are good" and "non-Christians are evil" may even (unintentionally) be passed on to his own children someday.

How many other religious children grow up with the same false, simplistic generalizations in the back of their minds?

Imagine this scenario playing out as the child gets older: He meets an atheist in high school and realizes that her eternal soul may be in jeopardy. So he begins to evangelize. He goes into a well-rehearsed speech about how Jesus can save her from a life of depravity, harmful drugs, destructive decisions, and, of course, unibrows.

At best, the atheist in that situation would probably be confused because those descriptions don't apply to most of us. I've met thousands of non-believers and, while there are always exceptions to the rule, I've found just about all of them to be law-abiding, family-loving, hard-working, good-natured human beings who try their best to live by the Golden Rule.

Can these two people have productive discussions? Can they be friends? If the person I'm talking to has that many misconceptions about who I am and what I believe (or don't), do I even *want* to have conversations with him?

Nicole Smalkowski and Jessica Ahlquist were both treated like the Evil Gingerbread Man by students who (I really want to believe) had the best of intentions but who came off sounding like bullies: antagonistic and mean.

There's a way to fix that mentality, though, and it involves a re-education of who atheists really are. Young atheists—even those without the comfort of a student group—are in the best position to deliver that lesson. That may be the most important reason we have to defend their right to be open and honest about their beliefs in their schools.

We've already seen the challenges that come from administrators who block the formation of atheist groups, but forming a group is only one way in which atheists can express themselves. In most cases, young atheists are on their own. Yet, they still face pressure to keep silent about their non-religious identities by the people closest to them, specifically their peers and their parents. Let's talk about each of these situations separately.

Sometimes other students can be a young atheist's toughest critics. When Devin Leaman began the Secular Student Alliance at Redlands High School in California, everything seemed to run smoothly at first. The principal supported them. Devin found a faculty sponsor eager and willing to help out. He had also found other students willing to take on leadership roles in the group. It almost sounded too easy.

Weeks before the first meeting, Devin and his officers posted more than one hundred flyers around the school to advertise their group, but by the time the final bell rang, only three were still up.

When Devin went to class that day, he heard another student saying, "Yeah, I tore a few of their flyers down and threw them away. They need to leave us alone."[1] Devin, undeterred by the incident, didn't tattle on the students. He simply forged ahead and held the meeting. Then, he held another. And another. As they met, and as other students realized what the group was trying to do (have conversations, educate others about atheism), the harassment came to a halt as well.

The initial opposition Devin faced isn't unique. When I asked the leader of a Secular Student Alliance high school group in Tennessee if his group had faced any problems, his response was curt: "Just the standard flyer vandalism." It's such a common problem among atheist groups that some of them make plans to put up flyers before *and* after school, knowing most of their signs won't be around by the end of the day.

Sometimes, the harassment is much more serious. When Allison Page was in second grade in Ohio, she read some Bible stories for the first time and thought they were pretty "silly." Take Cain and Abel, for example: "It just doesn't make sense... A brother wouldn't kill his brother."[2] But those kinds of simple questions went ignored by the students at her school, overshadowed by the bigger "problem" of Allison questioning the Bible at all. Many of her friends stopped talking to her altogether. One girl pushed her against the wall, holding Allison's shoulders in place, and told her she would go to hell if she didn't repent. When the bully let go, it was only to make a cross gesture with her fingers across Allison's chest. Allison was bound to tell her parents what had happened, so the bully warned her against it: "I'll hurt them" if you tell, she warned her victim.

Despite the threat, Allison told her mother. When the school couldn't guarantee Allison's safety, her mother Amy decided to homeschool her instead. One could argue that Amy should've fought to improve conditions at the school, but she felt that would only make the bullying worse and she didn't want to put Allison through that.

Things slowly began to get better for Allison away from the schoolyard. In fact, at a homeschooling event a couple of years later, Allison told a friend that she was an atheist. The friend responded back, "Hey, that's really cool! I am, too!" For several years, Allison also attended Camp Quest, a summer camp for children of atheist parents and a place where she could use the "A" word freely.

In the fall of 2012, Allison was set to enter high school, where she planned to start a Secular Student Alliance chapter. "I want to be able to create a group not just for me but for others, to be able to express themselves and not have to censor themselves," she said.[3]

Allison was fortunate that her mother was also an atheist. She didn't have to think twice about telling her mother the truth about what had happened at school as a result of stating her disbelief in Bible stories. Not every student is that fortunate.

My own experience makes me wonder how I would have fared in Allison's situation. My family moved to the south suburbs of Chicago the week before I began high school. I had just moved away from my best friends and I walked into a school with over three thousand students not knowing a single person. It was an incredibly tough time in my life. What made things more bearable—and eventually wonderful—was taking part in a school play and joining a competitive team, both of which introduced me to people who would quickly become close friends. At the time, I was still religious and my beliefs weren't a barrier in getting to know other students, but I worry about what would've happened if some integral part of my identity prevented other students from wanting to be around me.

In many communities where religion is a pervasive force, young atheists are either isolated if they're "out of the closet" or forced to keep their beliefs under wraps. Both options hinder their self-development. And what if they're not atheists? What if they're only *questioning* their beliefs? At a time when society ought to be encouraging that kind of thinking, there is significant pressure for these students to just "have faith." Stifling their curiosity won't solve anything, though.

Even if they don't want to form a club for atheists, they should be able to talk about their beliefs with their classmates in a way that doesn't inspire fear or hatred.

JT Eberhard, the former high school specialist at the Secular Student Alliance, explained it to me this way:

The biggest problem confronting these young atheists is hopelessness. *Things won't get better, so why try?* There is societal pressure to conform to the religious mindset of the other students, even if you don't believe as they do. For high-schoolers, social capital is the most important thing in the world and you risk losing it by admitting you're an atheist. Students are so inundated with this pressure that they don't always realize what an injustice this is.[4]

Even when young atheists and their classmates disagree on theology, we need to foster a climate where religious discussion is encouraged, stereotypes are busted, and questions are welcomed. Young atheists are well-equipped to promote all these ideas on their campuses and they may not even know it. In fact, they might shy away from being that voice of reason because they fear alienating so many people close to them.

We know being "different" is never easy in high school, but the bright side to having a unique identity at that age is that it's possible your classmates could also be more tolerant of you than the public at large. There's a very good reason younger generations tend to support same-sex marriage at a rate far higher than the general public: When you know people who are gay, you're less likely to think there's something "wrong" with them.[5] Similarly, if young atheists can make themselves known to their classmates, there's a good chance atheism will become more acceptable—and significantly less demonized—as they all grow older.

There's also a better chance people won't see all atheists as evil clothes-ripping drug abusers with no moral decency.

I can say from experience that some of my closest friendships in high school and college formed with religious people because we both enjoyed debating the topic. We could talk about faith and challenge each other, never with malice. I didn't treat them like they were idiots and they never spoke to me like they were trying to earn a spiritual merit badge. Without those conversations, I would've missed out on the chance to solidify my own views—and prepare myself for the arguments theists have often thrown my way ever since. I hope my friends remember those conversations as fondly as I do.

As we've seen from the large number of students who have tried to start groups at their schools, there are students willing to "out" themselves as atheists despite the potential pushback from their peers. But there's another obstacle that may seem far more insurmountable.

Parents have the unique ability to put a stop to religious discussion before it even begins. When religious parents find out their children are atheists, the response can often range anywhere from not allowing them to participate in the school's atheist club to kicking them out of the house.

One group of high school students in Tennessee told me how they managed to get a good turnout for their Secular Student Alliance group meetings despite all members needing to bring a permission slip signed by their parents: Many members just forged the signatures. They knew their parents would never allow them to take part in a forum where they could openly express their religious doubts.

They shouldn't have to resort to that.

It's not surprising to see them do it, though, when you hear about how some religious parents react to their children's atheism.

Chelsea, a recent graduate of Collingswood High School in New Jersey, chose to take a public stand as an atheist when she saw her school district violating the law. Now, her parents want little to do with her.

In 2012, Chelsea remained seated as her classmates recited the Pledge of Allegiance. Under the law, she had every right to do this. However, the Code of Conduct in her district mandated that all students had to "show proper respect to the flag by standing and removing any head dress." Chelsea stayed put, anyway.[6] That's when her teacher began to take issue with it, telling her she faced "possible disciplinary action"—three detentions to be exact[7]—if she didn't stand. Knowing that the district's Code of Conduct was illegal, Chelsea informed the New Jersey Law Revision Commission about what was happening. They told her she was right and provided her with documentation to show her administrators. Faced with the evidence, the administrators agreed to drop the punishments against her... but they told her "not [to] show it to anyone else or [she] would again face punishment." So Chelsea informed the local media. The pressure from the news station forced the district's superintendent to say he would revise the Code of Conduct the following year.

This is *exactly* the type of activism we want to see from secular students. When they see something wrong, they should act on it. Chelsea deserves awards from atheist and church/state separation organizations and applause from the rest of us for doing what she did.

The news story was pretty sympathetic to Chelsea and what she had done.[8] But what happened after the cameras went away?

While Chelsea received a lot of positive feedback on the Internet, much of the negative feedback came from her own family. She told me:

> Many of them have ceased communicating with me or have insisted that I am a 'idiotic and worthless child' that needs to repent... The worst part of this entire thing is that I was kicked out of my house the day I graduated. My father's girlfriend refused to have an atheist living with her. She thought God would set the place on fire I guess.[9]

Chelsea was forced to rent a place of her own, a place she now pays for by working ten-hour shifts at a local warehouse.

> I was planning on living at home for most of college. But the cards are dealt, I have to play with

what I have now. I know it will be better in the end
because I don't have to hide who I am anymore.

Are there any religious parents out there *condoning* this
type of treatment? If not, why does this happen?

Chelsea's not the only person who suffered a draconian
punishment for correctly challenging her district when no one
else would do it. Damon Fowler did something similar in 2011.

Damon was graduating from Louisiana's Bastrop High
School when he found out a prayer was part of the graduation
ceremony.[10] So he sent a letter to both the superintendent of the
Morehouse Parish School System in Louisiana and the principal
of Bastrop High School telling them the prayer was illegal and he
would contact the ACLU if he had to.[11] The principal complied,
but as soon as word got out, the trouble began for Damon.[12] One
of the faculty members even trashed him in the local media,
saying to a reporter, "… what's even more sad is this is a student
who really hasn't contributed anything to graduation or to their
classmates." [13] That faculty member added that other non-
religious students had remained silent about the prayer for
years—why couldn't Damon do the same?

Because Damon knew that "tradition" wasn't good
enough justification for letting bad practices go unchallenged.

A spokesperson for Americans United for Separation of
Church and State rebutted the teacher's argument by suggesting
that Damon *had* indeed contributed something of great
importance to his school:

> He's taught his fellow students that no matter how
> hard it is, they should stand up for what's right. He
> also represents all those who have been afraid to
> challenge the unconstitutional practice all these
> years.[14]

It was around this time that Damon's mother stopped
speaking to him.[15] When they found out he was an atheist (it was
hard to ignore that bit of information in all the news stories)

they also cut him off financially and threw his belongings out on the front porch.[16]

At the graduation ceremony, a prayer to Jesus was said, anyway. It was followed by a moment of silence (another opportunity for prayer) and the Pledge of Allegiance (with "Under God").[17] Damon had plenty of support from his online fans[18], but that didn't make up for the fact that his parents still didn't want him living with them.

All that for challenging his high school's graduation prayers.

For what it's worth, Damon's challenge eventually prevailed as Bastrop High School's graduation ceremony in 2012 went on without a moment of silence or a graduation prayer.[19] Unfortunately, Damon wasn't around to see the fruits of his labor in person. He was living with his brother in Texas, away from his parents.

It may seem like I'm being unfair in sharing these particular stories, but they're not just extreme examples of religious parents. I suspect there would be even more stories like these... but we don't hear about them because their children don't want to tell them about their religious views.

I spoke with a girl in Texas who was eager to start an atheist club at her school in order to meet others who shared her views—but she couldn't bring herself to do it because she was afraid her Baptist parents would find out.[20]

I asked her what would happen if her parents learned of her atheism:

> They would probably ground me and take away my means of communication, such as my cell phone, claiming that 'outside influences'... were what caused my disbelief... They would enforce strict rules on entertainment, believing that the books I read, the music I listen to, and television I watch are 'bad influences'... I'd be shut off from the world and possibly forced to go to counseling... They could always surprise me by reacting much

more rationally, but their actions in the past lead
me to assume the worst.[21]

Before I go on, I just want to clarify a point. *What are
these parents so afraid of?* They're afraid of a false stereotype.
They're afraid of the Evil Gingerbread Man. They're afraid their
children will suddenly lose all sense of morality and ethics and
kindness and decency—and that couldn't be further from the
truth! Unfortunately, they often punish their children by cutting
them off from the very communities that could help them
develop and act on these characteristics.

It's not only the parents of atheists who pose a challenge
to their children. Sometimes, the hurdle comes in the form of
other students' parents who don't want their own children to be
anywhere near the atheists.

In 2011, at Larkin High School in Elgin, Illinois, a couple of
students set up tables in the cafeteria (with permission from
their principal) in order to participate in Ask An Atheist Day, a
Secular Student Alliance-sponsored event in which atheists at
high schools and colleges are encouraged to answer questions
from their peers without acrimony or anger. The students didn't
proselytize or walk up to any of the students eating lunch. They
just sat at their table and waited for students to come to them.

When a local newspaper reported on this story—it must
have been a slow news day—one parent couldn't believe what
was happening:

> "They were here to talk about atheism," said
> Shavon Stanback of Elgin. "That's totally
> unacceptable to me."
>
> She continued: "I'm a Christian woman. I believe in
> God. I believe in heaven and hell."[22]

Apparently, she didn't believe in the students' right to
openly declare their non-Christianity... Amazingly, in a separate
story a month later, the *same parent* talked about the action step

her husband took when they heard about the atheists' table: They signed their kids out of school for the rest of the day.[23]

An Alternative Approach

What would happen to all these young atheists if their parents said, "I may disagree with you, but I still love you"? What would happen if they expressed their disappointment but added that they just wanted to make sure that the morals they raised their kids with were still intact? What would happen if they engaged in real discussions about faith and truth and what the church gets right and wrong—in a productive way?

It doesn't happen nearly enough. It's been said that you can't reason somebody out of something they were never reasoned into in the first place, and that sentiment is ignored when it comes to religious parents with atheist children. Instead of attempting to offer a rational explanation for why God must exist and why their particular brand of faith must be the correct one, many religious parents push their kids away or threaten them with punishment (in this life or the next). It only makes the relationship worse, but it doesn't have to be like that. It's possible to be both disappointed with your children for disagreeing with you but accepting of them at the same time. (It's also possible to be proud of them for coming to their own conclusions about such a weighty topic... but those stories are all too rare in my experience.)

If only other parents could be like those of a high school student from Arizona named Emma. She had always kept pretty quiet about her atheism due to shyness, but her mother told her she should begin an atheist group at her school. It was a way to meet like-minded people and become more comfortable in her identity. After Emma started the group, she did everything she could to confront the stigma associated with atheism, adding that the group "gave me the boost I needed to come out." Was her mother an atheist? It didn't matter. The important thing was that Emma benefitted from her group, becoming a stronger person as a result of it. It was good for the daughter, so it should have been good for the parents as well.

It's possible that religious parents worry that allowing their children to "run free" with atheism is akin to tacitly approving something destructive. But as we've seen all over the country, these groups are a positive force for their communities, encouraging discussion, participation in service projects, and critical thinking. If parents are worried about atheist groups, it's because of false stereotypes, not anything based in fact.

As a teacher, I *want* to see my students develop the kind of leadership Emma had, using the skills they're learning in the classroom. As a parent, I would want my children to be confident in their ability to ask questions, even if they might be taboo in some circles. As a student, I would want my friends to be happy, feeling no need to hide their beliefs from me.

Wanting young atheists to be open and honest about their beliefs shouldn't be controversial. But until the people in their lives stop running scared at the mere mention of their godlessness, we may never see their full potential.

All of the stories I'm sharing in this chapter are unusual. They're unusual because *we know about them*—they were discussed in the local press or mentioned on a website or shared with me directly. But for each of these stories, how many more do we miss? How many atheists have their groups dismissed, or their non-religious identities used against them, or their relationship with their parents fractured, all on account of what people *think* is wrong with them? How many atheists believe there's no way to fight back?

Before we talk about the solutions, though, there are still issues young atheists have to deal with that we haven't talked about. We know they have trouble starting groups. We know they have a hard time coming out as atheists. We know administrators, peers, and parents can stand in their way. But they also face a multitude of challenges from religious people who use the school system as an arm of their church, proselytizing and pushing their faith onto all students who are not yet "saved."

5

The Morning Bell

How Religion is Pushed into Public Schools

In many high schools today, the morning isn't complete without saying the Pledge of Allegiance. For a lot of students, this is a ritual that requires little thought: Stand up, say the words, sit down. For many atheists, though, it's not quite so casual. They have to ask whether they're being true to themselves if they say the Pledge, which includes the phrase "one nation under God." Do you stand up at all? Do you put your hand over your heart? Do you just say the Pledge without the "offending" phrase? If you do any of those things, what are your classmates going to say about you? Will the teacher punish you?

Even though saying the Pledge is voluntary, many lawsuits have been filed—usually unsuccessfully—to stop recitals of it, on the grounds that it's an unconstitutional endorsement of religion in the public schools. It's not a recent phenomenon, nor is it the only instance in which we've seen an homage to God in a classroom setting.

The situation for non-Christians was much worse in the 1950s. Pennsylvania, for example, had a law mandating that "at least ten verses from the Holy Bible shall be read, without comment, at the opening of each public school on each school day."[1]

If you had your parents' permission, you could be excused from the Bible-readings, but that didn't mean the recitation was legal. And that wasn't all the state made children do, either. The Bible verses were followed by the Lord's Prayer, adding yet another dose of Christianity to a religion-filled morning. And, since that apparently wasn't enough, the Pledge of Allegiance came right afterward. Other states had similar laws.

As a historical footnote, this was around the time the Cold War was being waged and "anti-Christian" Communism was seen as a threat to America. Legislators doubled down on their efforts to declare our country a good, God-fearing one. In 1952, Congress passed a resolution to mark the National Day of Prayer.[2] In 1954, it added the words "Under God" to the Pledge of Allegiance.[3] In 1956, it changed the country's motto to "In God We Trust."[4] In 1957, that motto was put on paper money.[5] With all that in mind, it's hardly a surprise that Bible verses were a part of the morning ritual in many public schools.

Ellery Schempp grew up in this era. When he was in elementary school, his teacher read Bible verses to the students. By ninth grade, students were told to read aloud from the Bible. Ellery, just to make light of the situation, read from the erotic Song of Songs. "The teacher did not like it, but what could he say? It's in the Bible," Ellery would later joke.[6]

In 1956, when Ellery was a junior at Abington Senior High School, situated in a suburb north of Philadelphia, he had come to understand the Bible readings weren't legal. Not only that, but he grew up in a Unitarian church and he didn't believe what the King James Version of the Bible—the one they used at his school—said. So on November 26, the Monday after Thanksgiving break, he came to Abington High ready to execute a plan. If he had to sit through a "Morning Devotional," he was going to read something—*anything*—explicitly non-Christian, just to make the point that there were other holy books out there and the Bible was no different, no more special, and no more truthful. He also figured he was immune from punishment since he was a strong student:

> I was aware of the Hindu Upanishads and Bhagavad Gita, and the Buddhist Sutras, but did not have a copy. My friend George mentioned that his father had a Koran in his library...

I did not have much fear. I knew I had the support of my parents and a number of close [high school] friends. I knew that McCarthyism was waning. And I thought, *what could they do to me?* I was an A student; they could hardly suspend me on a matter of conscience.[7]

When the time came for the morning's Bible readings, Ellery opened the Islamic text he had borrowed from his friend's dad and began quietly leafing through it. Then, as the Lord's Prayer sounded through the loudspeaker afterward, he stayed in his seat. Ellery recalled what happened after that:

The reaction was swift. My homeroom teacher demanded to know what was going on. I replied that as a matter of religious conscience, I could no longer participate in these devotions. It is fair to say that he was pretty much speechless. But he knew disobedience when he saw it.[8]

Ellery was sent to the principal's office. He tried to make his case that the prayers went against the First Amendment, but the principal wasn't having it. *Respect others*, the principal said. Ellery retorted: *I respect the First Amendment.* That earned him a meeting with the school guidance counselor, who asked him if he was having problems at home (he wasn't). Ellery was eventually sent back to class without punishment, but he wasn't done just yet. That night, with the approval of his parents, he sent a letter to the ACLU:

November 26, 1956

Gentlemen:

As a student in my junior year at Abington Senior High School, I would very greatly appreciate any information that you might send regarding possible Union action and/or aid in testing the constitutionality of Pennsylvania law, which arbitrarily (and seemingly unrighteously and unconstitutionally) compels the Bible to be read in our public school system. I thank you for any help you might offer in freeing American youth in Pennsylvania from this gross violation of their religious rights as guaranteed in the first and foremost Amendment in our United States' Constitution.

Sincerely yours,

Ellery F. Schempp[9]

Just to make sure they would read it, Ellery enclosed a ten-dollar bill (quite a lot of money at the time) with his letter. The attention-getter must have worked because the ACLU soon filed a lawsuit that would remain in the court system for nearly seven years. When Ellery graduated, his younger siblings became the plaintiffs, allowing the family to still have standing in the case. In 1963, after Ellery had graduated from college, the case culminated in an 8-1 victory in the Supreme Court, ending devotional Bible readings and school-sponsored prayers across the country.[10]

As the case ran its course through the courts, Ellery and his siblings dealt with a lot of negative attention:

> ... my brother Roger was kicked around a few times; kids shouted 'now passing the commie camp' from the school bus. My sister Donna was mortified, and some parents told their daughters not to play with her. I later learned that my principal wrote letters of disrecommendation to every college I applied to.

Even decades later, Ellery's younger sister Donna remembered how tough it was for her when the courts were deciding how to handle the school prayers:

> I think the Bible reading case put a lot of strain on our family. It was the center of our lives for many years, between letters from people, phone calls, etc. It put a lot of strain on [brother] Roger and me who were attending school and being taunted by kids because of it. I, in particular, was embarrassed by it. It was a time when I wanted to be just like everyone else and this, by definition, singled me out. So, although I supported it intellectually, I hated it emotionally. It has taken me a lot of time to recover from that embarrassment and sometimes I get scared, like I was worried how my mother-in-law would react if she found out about it—a little old lady in Iowa who is very religious.[11]

It would've been worse, Ellery says, if his family members were atheists. The Unitarian label they used spared them some of the wrath atheist Madalyn Murray and her family faced as they went through their own court challenge (later merged with the Schempps' case) to get Bible readings removed from public schools.[12]

Although this case occurred several decades ago, this is a sentiment shared by many of the students who challenge unlawful intrusions of religion into their schools today. They know what they're doing is right, but the social pressures can take an emotional toll. While it would be ideal to take a stand knowing your friends are going to back you up, that's almost never the case. The plaintiffs tend to have two choices in these cases: Stay silent and remain accepted, or speak up and become isolated.

At least Ellery and his siblings had the support of their parents. Very few atheists are brave enough to stand up against what they see as violations of their rights; even fewer have encouragement from their families.

Promotion of Religion in Public Schools Is Still Happening

Almost fifty years after mandatory Bible readings in public schools were deemed unconstitutional by the Supreme Court, young atheists today still face a barrage of God in school in a number of ways.

In some cases, the preferential treatment of Christianity is so under-the-radar, you wouldn't even know it unless you turned on the school computers and tried to log onto a website that discussed atheism favorably, only to discover you're unable to access it because it's blocked by the school's Internet filters. Indeed, some schools will not allow you to access websites about "alternative spirituality/belief," which eliminates websites discussing atheism or Wiccan, while still allowing access to Christianity-focused websites. [13] (Strangely enough, atheist websites have also been banned under the "occult" category.[14])

In other cases, public schools may even partner with churches who provide tutoring services or free lunches for students while they attend Vacation Bible School during the summer.[15] These are taxpayer-funded, government-sponsored incentives to encourage students to become (or at least pretend to become) Christians.

Some districts have also tried to push Christian beliefs into public schools by posting a Ten Commandments plaque on the walls—with or without other kinds of "moral codes" surrounding it.[16]

Those forms of religious discrimination, unlike what happened in Ellery Schempp's case, don't necessarily shine a spotlight on specific atheist students by themselves. But this behavior in the public schools—promoting Christianity in such a way that non-Christians are made to be outcasts through no action of their own—has a much greater impact on the lives of individual atheists.

The Freedom From Religion Foundation, which fights these battles head-on, has seen a rise in these kinds of problems at public schools over the past few years. Only counting the offenses it can take action on (by writing a letter to the administration, for example), the number of school-related complaints has gone from 54 in 2009, to 130 in 2010, to 310 in 2011, to an estimated 600 in 2012.[17]

Of the many concerns regarding illegal promotion of Christianity in public schools, the violation that comes up *more than any other* is prayer at a graduation or athletic event. Not private, personal prayers, but public ones that are theoretically meant to include everyone... yet never do. Nearly five decades after Ellery Schempp's court victory, prayer is still a problem in public schools.

God at Graduation

In 1984, James Brodhead noticed that God played a prominent role in his son's graduation ceremony at California's Van Nuys High School. When he asked the principal to stop the prayers in the future, he received no promise that the school would. So, one month prior to his second son's graduation in 1986, Brodhead filed a lawsuit against the district. A couple of weeks later, the board agreed in writing that it wouldn't allow "any language or other behavior that constitutes a religious observance or practice." [18] A generic invocation would be allowed, as would a "statement of thanksgiving," but no explicit prayer or mention of God.[19]

Did it stop anyone from praying privately? Of course not. But you wouldn't have known it based on the reactions from local Christians. Reverend Lou Sheldon of the California Coalition for Traditional Values spent four hundred dollars for a plane to fly over the ceremony with a banner on its tail reading, "God Bless the Graduates '86." As the Pledge of Allegiance was said, dozens of students yelled the "Under God" part. And protesters stood outside the ceremony gates with signs for Brodhead's son,

Daniel, reading: "Congratulations Atheist." (How sweet of them...)

It wasn't any easier in 1999 for Nick Becker, a senior from Maryland, who acquired the nickname "Young Atheist of Calvert County" for his opposition to the graduation prayer at Northern High School. (Nick was actually Agnostic, but it was a meaningless distinction for his critics.)

Nick was a student who understood and appreciated rules and logic. He took two math classes a year all throughout high school and helped create a website to help other students with calculus. As a junior, Nick attended his school's graduation ceremony to watch his friend walk across the stage. He was surprised to hear a student leading the crowd in a Christian prayer, saying later, "I thought, 'They can't do this; it's not legal.'" It wasn't the first time he had those thoughts, either. Earlier in the year, he remained seated during the Pledge of Allegiance and was sent to the principal's office as a result. Threatened with a suspension, he emailed the ACLU, which sent the school a message that what Nick had done was perfectly legal. The principal quickly apologized.

Now a senior, Nick went back to his principal armed with documentation that the Christian graduation prayer was illegal. The ACLU and the Attorney General of Maryland agreed with him, too. So the principal, faced with the facts, agreed to remove the prayer from the ceremony.

When the school community discovered that formal prayer would be banned from the ceremony, Nick had to deal with the blowback. One student, referring to Nick, shouted in the hallway, "He doesn't respect the flag; he doesn't respect anything!" Conservative writer Cal Thomas compared Nick to Columbine High School shooters Eric Harris and Dylan Klebold in his syndicated column.[20]

By the time the graduation rolled around, the furor hadn't died down. During the moment of silent reflection that was substituted in place of the prayer, some audience members said the Lord's Prayer anyway, including elected officials. Nick walked out of the ceremony at that point and tried to return just to get his diploma—but state police threatened to arrest him. He tried to go on the post-graduation boat cruise since he had bought a ticket, but he was barred from that celebration, too.

His mother Patti knew some of this would happen, but she wasn't expecting the vitriol to rise to the level that it did. Even though her parents (Nick's grandparents) flew in from Florida to watch Nick graduate, Patti lied to them and said she was unable to get tickets, so they would have to stay home during the ceremony. Patti didn't want them to experience what she knew would be a disappointing event for Nick. As she reflected on her son having to deal with the police just to obtain his diploma, she couldn't believe what he was put through:

> "This is the most horrible experience we've been through," says Patti Becker, who has had trouble sleeping since the episode. "We were going to see our son, who excelled in high school, at his graduation, and what we ended up with was total humiliation. We're not prepared for this. It's painful, whether Nick was right or wrong. It's painful to see your child called a lone malcontent and atheist, splashed across the papers." The sight of her son in a police squad car was too much. "I just collapsed and started crying," Patti Becker said.

After the ceremony, Nick's parents sent him to San Francisco just so he could get out of town for a week.[21]

All that for saying that Christian prayers had no business being a formal part of a public school's graduation ceremony. Is it any wonder that atheists are often hesitant to speak out?

In some schools, the administrators understand that they cannot lead the crowd in a Christian prayer. They also know that *students* cannot lead the crowd in a Christian prayer. For district officials who want prayer in the ceremony regardless, there are a couple of ways to work around those "barriers." One method is to allow certain students (valedictorians, class presidents, etc.)

to give speeches *without screening them in advance*—essentially telling those students that if they bring God into their speeches, they will not be punished because officials will look the other way. Another method is to allow the students to *vote* on whether or not prayers should be included in the ceremony. Since the administrators are almost certainly aware that the majority of the students are Christians who will vote in favor of the prayer, this is a deviously clever method to let the public believe prayer is what the *students* wanted, when, in reality, it was the administrators who allowed it to happen. Because of that, this method is easily challenged in the courts. Even though it's technically student-led, it's letting the majority impose its will on the minority instead of keeping the graduation a religiously-neutral event for everybody.

Eric Workman encountered both of these methods the year he graduated from Greenwood Community High School in Indiana, ten years after Nick Becker fought his battle. In September of 2009, Eric and his fellow seniors were called into the school auditorium to talk about the coming year. On the agenda: Every student was to vote on whether or not to have a non-denominational prayer at the graduation ceremony. The principal and other staff members handed out the ballots to the students and Eric, knowing this was an illegal school endorsement of religion, voted "No."[22] Additionally, he included a note on the back of his ballot that he would be contacting the ACLU if the school went through with the prayer.[23]

Either no one noticed or paid much attention to the note because the school moved forward with plans for a non-denominational prayer. On March 11, 2010, the ACLU filed a lawsuit against the school on Eric's behalf. Approximately six weeks later, the judge issued her ruling: "The degree of school involvement ma[de] it clear that [any graduation] prayer [would] 'bear the mark of the state,' and accordingly [transgress] the Constitution." It sounded like the school had lost the case and the prayers would come to an end.

But they didn't. The school implemented a new policy in the wake of the judge's decision. Administrators told the student speakers (*wink wink*) that they would not be reviewing students' speeches in advance (*nudge nudge*)—even if they used profane language or injected their political beliefs into the speeches.[24] Without explicitly saying it, it was the easiest way to get Christ into a speech without directly implicating the administrators.

Indeed, the class president took advantage of everyone looking the other way. She gave thanks to God, adding that "None of us would even be alive, and I personally wouldn't be standing here, without him." In addition, she read a verse from the Bible and told the audience, "People come and go, but God is always there for you... I believe he deserves to be thanked for that."[25]

Even if the legality of not pre-screening speeches was in question, a student praising God in the way that she did was entirely legal. The crowd loved it. They cheered and applauded any mention of God.

Then, it was Eric's turn. As the class valedictorian, he was one of the student speakers at the ceremony, and he had reason to believe students would protest his speech. At the very least, one student told a reporter what his classmates planned to do:

> "Someone is going to sneeze, and everyone [will say], 'God bless you,' in order to get back at Eric Workman," said Nick Rice, a junior at the school.[26]

It may have been a mild protest, but it was clear that Eric wasn't going to get the same level of respect as the other speakers.

Eric also took advantage of the school's no-screening policy, focusing his speech on his battle and the unnecessary fight his administration picked with the Constitution:

> In September of last year, our remarkably doltish administration called upon us all to vote in deciding whether or not we wanted the Constitution of the United States to be flagrantly violated. Understanding the law and knowing right

from wrong, I vehemently opposed such an atrocious act from ever taking place. However, my one voice and the voices of others were shouted down by most of you. Our rights and the law were disregarded. You see, subjecting government-endorsed prayer to a majority rule is, in and of itself, unconstitutional, let alone the government approbation of said prayer. Founding Father Thomas Jefferson is quoted as having said, "All, too, will bear in mind this sacred principle, that though the will of the majority is in [most] cases to prevail, that will to be rightful must be reasonable; that the minority possess their equal rights, which equal law must protect, and to violate [them] would be oppression."[27]

There were "signs of disapproval" from the audience, according to one reporter, and the obligatory applause afterward was much more tepid than it was for the other speakers.[28]

It's worth noting that, during this entire battle, Eric was a Christian. Even though he was religious, he understood why religion and government needed to be kept separate. It was only after experiencing the backlash from his religious classmates that he began his journey to atheism.

When all was said and done, the school district not only wasted money on its own legal representation, it also owed the ACLU $14,500 in court costs.

Though some Christians accused Eric of raising a fuss about the prayers in order to make money, it was a baseless accusation. Eric's portion of the settlement amounted to a grand total of one dollar.[29]

Looking back at what he accomplished, Eric now feels that he came out of the experience as a "much stronger and more resolved individual."[30]

Is there a long-lasting consequence to taking such a courageous stance? Absolutely, and in this case, those results were positive. Greenwood Community High School no longer allows students to vote on graduation prayers.[31] And Eric's willingness to take a stand on this issue inspired another student to do the same thing.

As a junior, Harrison Hopkins was aware that his class in South Carolina's Laurens County School District 55 would also be voting on graduation prayers the following year.[32] He watched Eric's case closely and, when Eric earned a court victory, Harrison gained confidence that he, too, could challenge his district.

In April of 2011, a week before the prayer vote was to take place, Harrison contacted the Freedom From Religion Foundation to discuss his situation. Immediately, FFRF took action, sending the principal and superintendent a letter describing the infraction they were committing and the consequences if they followed through with it. It appeared that Harrison had blunted any attempt at a graduation prayer. However, at the senior class meeting when the vote would have taken place, Harrison and the other students received a handout stating that their graduation ceremony would not be complete until "after the prayer and recessional."

Harrison once again contacted FFRF, and once again, FFRF sent the district a letter.

By this time, word had spread throughout the school that Harrison had gotten prayer "banned" from graduation. And the cycle we've become so used to seeing for young atheist activists began anew. On Facebook, Harrison received threats like "Now I'm no fan of senseless violence, but... this kid needs to be taken out back and have his ass kicked to beat some sense into him." Students called him "devil boy" and "antichrist." Rumors circulated that Harrison would get beaten up but, thankfully, nothing like that transpired. (A few students told Harrison they supported what he was doing.)[33]

And then, on graduation day, the situation played out in a way eerily similar to Eric Workman's. Even though the students didn't vote on a prayer, the students' speeches were purposely not pre-screened by the administrators.

The student body president opened up his speech by saying, "I'd like to thank our administration, our teachers, our parents, but there's one more person I'd like to thank, and that person is God. Will you join me in prayer?" The crowd ate it up.

Once again, at a ceremony that was supposed to be a day of celebration for everyone involved, religion needlessly divided the crowd, and the one student who had the courage to speak out against his district's pro-religion policy was made to feel excluded. Harrison was the focus of every pair of eyes angry about the fact that formal prayers were not a part of the ceremony. Still, his belief that doing what was *right* was more important than doing what was *popular* should serve as a guide for all young students, atheist and religious alike.

God at the Game

Athletic events with prayers are usually stopped fairly quickly, thanks to a Supreme Court decision from 2000. In *Santa Fe Independent School District v Doe*, the Court ruled 6-3 that prayers at high school football games, even student-led and student-initiated ones, are a violation of the Establishment Clause of the First Amendment.[34]

Maybe news of that decision didn't reach the folks at Soddy-Daisy High School in Tennessee. In 2010, they were still saying prayers over the loudspeakers before the start of football games. A student at the school had tried speaking with administrators but they ignored him. The ACLU tried to step in, but the organization understandably wanted his parents' permission before they pursued the case; the parents wouldn't give the ACLU the permission it needed. Eventually, FFRF investigated the charges and sent the school a letter of complaint: Even though the pre-game invocations were student-initiated, that didn't make them legal.[35]

Not surprisingly, the community wasn't very happy. Board of Education member Rhonda Thurman was a firm supporter of the prayers and believed all non-Christians could just "put their fingers in their ears."

"Everybody is offended by something," she said.
"I'm offended by a lot of those little girls running
around with their thong panties showing, but I
can't make that go away."[36]

Sure, people can be offended by just about anything and
we can't always stop that from happening. But there's a marked
difference between taking offense and violating others' civil
liberties. A blogger for Americans United for Separation of
Church and State echoed that sentiment:

Claiming that students can just "put their fingers in
their ears" doesn't change the fact that the school
is unfairly and unconstitutionally favoring one
particular religion. Students of all faiths and none
should feel welcome at school. They should not
feel like outcasts because school officials forget
that it's their duty is to remain neutral on the topic
of religion. Parents should determine what faith
their children practice, not school officials.

Students have the right to voluntarily practice
their faith in public schools so long as it does not
disrupt others or interrupt class time. But school
officials cannot give preferential treatment to one
religious belief by allowing only Christian prayers
to be broadcast over the loudspeakers.[37]

The superintendent eventually told FFRF that public
prayers would no longer be allowed at school events. The whole
time, the student who alerted FFRF about the violations in the
first place kept a low profile, remaining anonymous and making
no public comments afterward "because of all the hate. It may
have become a safety issue for my family if I were to talk to
anyone."[38]

No students should be put in that position because the adults around them don't know the difference between church and school.

Football games in particular seem to be a magnet for religious proselytizing. In addition to the loudspeaker prayers, head coaches have taken on the role of team pastors. [39] In the fall of 2012, Mark Mariakis, the head football coach at Georgia's Ridgeland High School, was accused of leading prayers for the team, taking them to a local church for pregame meals, putting Bible verses on team gear (like shirts), pressuring students to attend Christian football camps, and appointing a team chaplain.[40]

Sometimes, other athletes get involved, too. In 2009, the cheerleaders at Lakeview-Fort Oglethorpe High School in Georgia used Bible verses on the run-through banners the football burst through prior to the start of their home games.[41] It took a Christian parent's complaint to finally put a stop to the five-year-old practice.[42] In the fall of 2012, cheerleaders in the Kountze Independent School District in Texas were guilty of the same sort of religious promotion.[43]

All of these instances go beyond personal prayers or, say, Tebowing. They're pushing religion to the crowd and other athletes at school-sponsored events. I suspect that if these promotions involved atheism or a non-Christian faith, they would be shut down immediately. Yet, when Christians are at the center of the story, the practices continue and we rehash the same issues season after season.

God in the Classroom

The Pledge of Allegiance and prayers at school-sponsored events are unfortunately not the only ways religion gets into the school system.

Sometimes, it happens directly in the classroom. And I'm not even talking about efforts to inject Creationism or Intelligent Design into science curricula.

In 2011, a teacher in the South Texas Independent School District put up a nativity scene in his classroom—in his words, "for people of my faith, fellow Christians." For the non-Christians, he put up a different display: "The Grinch Who Stole Christmas." When a student confronted him about it, the teacher kicked the student out of class.[44]

Bradley Johnson, a math teacher at Westview High School in California, had Christian banners hanging from his classroom for decades because no one had the guts to tell the proper authorities about it. One of the signs, up for twenty-five years, consisted of four lines in alternating red, white, and blue colors reading:

In God We Trust
One Nation Under God
God Bless America
God Shed His Grace on Thee

The other, up for seventeen years, read "All Men Are Created Equal" and "They Are Endowed By Their CREATOR."[45]

It took a ruling from the U.S. 9th Circuit Court of Appeals to force Johnson to take those signs down.[46]

One of his former students (not involved in this lawsuit) told me his signs made her feel "unwelcome in his classroom" despite being a strong student. She felt that if Johnson ever found out about her atheism, she could lose any approval she had earned through her work in his class.[47] Who knows how many other non-Christian students felt alienated or silenced in all the years he had those signs up?

Sometimes, God is pushed into music classes and choir performances.[48] Obviously, it's legal to study religious music and there's no doubt that God plays a prominent role in the classical canon. However, there are limits. If the bulk of the songs sung in a choral program are explicitly Christian, it can be illegal, even during holiday performances. If your public high school is singing contemporary Christian songs at an event, like the Houston County Schools in Georgia did in 2012, that is almost certainly breaking the law.[49] It could be argued that choir directors who choose these songs are either forcing non-Christian kids to sing songs that go against their faith or forcing them to exclude themselves from their peers. A program consisting of songs from a variety of religious and non-religious traditions is legal and preferred.

Unfortunately, challenging an overly-religious choral program can be just as daunting as fighting graduation prayers.

Briana Lamet was a junior at Concord High School in Delaware in 2010 when she took a stand against her choir director. She was a talented singer, making both the Delaware All-State Senior Chorus and her school's audition-only choral group. What finally got her to take a stand against her director was the increasingly religious music they were singing in school. For example, her high school's holiday concert selections that year had a very obvious theme: "Ave Maria," "Dormi Jesu," "Love Psalm," "The Lord Bless You and Keep You," "Break Forth O Beauteous Heavenly Light," "If Ye Love Me (Keep My Commandments)," "Cantate Domino," and others. Despite the variety of languages, Briana said, the songs were overwhelmingly Christian "with strong, clear Jesus-loving messages."[50]

This was simply unacceptable in a public school. A collection of songs from a variety of religious backgrounds might have been okay, but this was crossing the line. Furthermore, the way the director talked about the songs, she began to feel like the class was more like a cult than a chorus.

There was no alternative for her, either. Briana offered to participate only in the secular pieces, but she wasn't allowed to do that or her grade would suffer. Then, she volunteered to learn other songs (so that she wasn't guilty of doing less work than the other students), but the director wouldn't give her that option, either. She had to sing all the songs or fail the class. When Briana told her principal about it, the response was to just drop the class—it was an elective, after all—but that wasn't fair to Briana. She had worked hard to make it into this chorus, and she didn't think she should have to drop the class because the teacher was doing something wrong.

Even though several other students in the class agreed with Briana that she should be exempted from the songs or the program needed to change, none of them wanted to speak up out of fear of being ostracized or kicked out of the prestigious chorus the following year. The one concession her director made was that Briana could visit other high schools choirs' shows and write essays about their performances and song choices, or write an essay about music in general. Both assignments may have been fine in a music theory class, but not in one where actual singing should have been the sole barometer for success.[51]

Finally, one of Briana's friends, someone who happened to be an atheist, told her she should contact the ACLU. Her state's legal director assured her this was a serious issue and offered to help. A letter explaining the problem with the current program was drafted and sent to the principal and superintendent, but in the interim between contacting the ACLU and it taking action on the matter, the concert took place. After everything she had done to change the program, Briana had to sing the overtly Christian songs anyway. Eventually, the principal and the ACLU agreed that they would review and comment on the following year's choral program together to guarantee that it respected students' varied religious affiliations. According to a press release put out by the ACLU of Delaware the following fall:

> Thanks to the principal's careful application of constitutional principles, with ACLU-DE's input, this year's choral students [will] have a musically sophisticated program that respects the First Amendment and American religious (and non-religious) diversity.[52]

The case never went to court, but it didn't have to. Still, later that spring, when Briana auditioned once again for her hard-to-make ensemble, the director didn't accept her.

During this whole process, Briana mostly got positive support from her friends who knew what had happened. The other students didn't know anything about the ACLU's involvement until the following year, and by that time, Briana's family had moved to another state (for unrelated reasons).

When the students found out many of their traditional holiday songs would no longer be part of the music program, the blame was cast on Briana, who wasn't even there to defend herself. Though she lived hours away, Briana began getting nasty messages on Facebook and Twitter. She also heard that she was getting mocked in class.

It didn't matter to her. She had made a real difference in her old school and prevented one religion from rearing its privilege. It's interesting to note that she didn't even call herself an atheist at the time. Still, she dared to question the religious influence being thrust upon her.

In retrospect, Briana is glad she stood up for herself. She knew a lot of students who supported what she did even though they didn't want to speak up themselves. They didn't want to be in the spotlight, but they gave Briana the encouragement not to give up.

Meanwhile, in her new school, Briana joined a choir that used its holiday concert to sing songs that were simply "fun" and not tied down to any one religious belief.

God at School Assemblies

I mentioned earlier that prayers at graduations and athletic events were the source of most of FFRF's school-related complaints. Next on the list are violations dealing with forming atheist groups, which we've already discussed. Third are religious groups brought in for school assemblies.

This happens more often than you might think. When planning an assembly to encourage students not to drink alcohol, take drugs, or partake in other potentially risky behaviors, schools often bring in religious groups to deliver the message, intentionally or not. The most egregious and high-profile example of this in recent memory took place in September of 2011 at New Heights Middle School in South Carolina. The school was a part of Chesterfield County, an area already home to two hundred Christian churches. You can understand why people might assume everyone in town was a Christian.

At the assembly, Pastor Christian Chapman delivered what might as well have been a sermon to the pre-teen students in the audience. Not only did he use his time to rail against atheism, evolution, and homosexuality, he told the students that "a relationship with Jesus is what you need, more important than anything else." Christian rapper Bryan Edmonds (a.k.a. B-SHOC) later joined him onstage and performed "overtly Christian songs" for the crowd. Even the principal joined the mix by telling students to attend a local church.

But that wasn't all. Students were told to sign a pledge dedicating themselves to Jesus Christ and teachers were told to pray with students before returning to the classroom. [53] Afterward, the public school's own website declared that "[b]efore the day ended, 324 kids had either been saved, or had re-committed their lives to the Lord."[54]

Jonathan Anderson was an atheist and his son was a seventh grader at the school. The son, also an atheist, had no intention of attending the assembly, knowing it would just make him uncomfortable, so he asked his teachers if he could skip it. They told him he could, but he would have to report to the room normally reserved for in-school suspensions, a place where students sat in silence and did extra work.[55] Faced with that alternative, the son attended the event. As his class prepared to go to the gym for the assembly, he told his teacher it wouldn't be very fun for him because he was an atheist. In response, the teacher told him, "I wouldn't brag about that."

All of this led Anderson to file a lawsuit against the school, with the help of the ACLU. This whole case could have been more difficult to prosecute if not for a video of the event posted on YouTube by B-SHOC himself, confirming many of the allegations.[56] (Eventually, the case was settled and the school agreed to put a stop to all the prayers, preaching, religious assemblies, and other religious activities directed at students.[57])

Again, we have to ask what the outcome of these events would have been had Mr. Anderson not stepped in on behalf of his son. It's possible the school would still be proselytizing to students today.

Katherine Stewart, the author of the previously-mentioned book *The Good News Club: The Christian Right's Stealth Assault on America's Children*, mentioned in her article "How religion is infiltrating public schools" that a number of groups brought in to make presentations at public schools are based in the religious world:

> The use of "character education" as a cover for religious proselytizing to public school children is now so common that it, too, has a nickname: "pizza evangelism." (It seems that the first missionaries to use the tactic tended to follow their character presentations with pizza parties.) Team Impact, Commandos! USA, the Power Team, Answering the Cries, Go to Tell Ministries, the Todd Becker Foundation, the Strength Team—these are just a few of the faith-based groups that enter public schools every year with presentations on drug addiction, drunk driving, and other important topics and aim to leave with a collection of young religious converts.[58]

This is what young atheists have to put up with all across the country. They are constantly faced with the decision of going along with the crowd when religion pushes its way into public schools or risk alienation from their peers. Even when they are courageous enough to speak out against it, they do so at their own peril. It's incredible to me that these students often know more about our Constitution than the very adults who are supposed to be teaching them about it. It's also worrisome that some teachers hesitate to speak up and "stir trouble" out of fear of losing their jobs.

Ellery Schempp had no fear when he brought a copy of the Koran to school because he knew he was doing the right thing and it didn't matter to him what others thought. We're the lucky beneficiaries of Ellery's courage. But becoming public figures or social pariahs isn't required to make a difference. In fact, young atheists can take specific steps to make things better for themselves and others like them.

6

Homework

What Atheists Can Do to Make a Difference

When Matthew LaClair began his junior year of high school in the fall of 2006, friends of his older sister Katie asked him who his teachers were going to be. They had graduated from Kearny High School in New Jersey only two years prior, so they knew the teachers' reputations—who was good, bad, helpful, strict, easy, etc. Matthew was eager to find out what he was in for, so he was more than happy to run his schedule by them. As he read through the list, one name stood out to them more than any other: David Paszkiewicz, his History teacher. They warned Matthew that Paszkiewicz (pronounced pass-KEV-ich) was someone who frequently brought his personal religious and political beliefs into the classroom.[1]

Almost immediately, Matthew understood what they meant. During the first week of school alone, Paszkiewicz, a devout Christian and youth pastor, told the class that biblical prophecies had come true, that dinosaurs were on Noah's Ark (which also implied that Noah's Ark *existed*), that evolution and the Big Bang were nonsense, that Creationism explained how humans came into this world, and that only Christians would have a space reserved in heaven:

> If you reject [Jesus'] gift of salvation, then you know where you belong... He did everything in his power to make sure that you could go to heaven, so much so that he took your sins on his own body, suffered your pains for you, and he's saying,

"Please, accept me, believe." If you reject that, you belong in hell.[2]

Was it possible that Paszkiewicz had been teaching for fourteen years without anyone speaking out against him? Did the administrators know about this? Should Matthew tell them what was going on? Would they believe him if he did?

Before he told the adults, Matthew knew he needed a way to offer them irrefutable proof of what he was hearing.

So on the third day of school, he came to class with his answer: An audio recorder, tucked safely inside his backpack. (New Jersey happened to be one of only a handful of states where recording a lecture without the teacher's knowledge was legal.[3]) On that day—and several more after that—Matthew recorded everything Paszkiewicz said. Not even his classmates knew what he was up to.

With his confidence boosted by the evidence he was gathering, Matthew wrote a letter to his principal expressing his concern about his teacher, stating, "I care about the future generation and I do not want Mr. Paszkiewicz to continue preaching to and poisoning students."[4] While he referenced some of the comments his teacher had made in class, he didn't mention the proof sitting in his backpack.

The principal spoke to Paszkiewicz about the issue and it seemed like the problem was resolved. That day, the teacher kept his personal views to himself. The students clearly noticed because one of them even asked him why he wasn't sharing his opinions as he usually did. Paszkiewicz responded by saying he didn't want his words taken out of context, a comment directed straight at Matthew. Still, Matthew said nothing, knowing his tape recorder was picking up the whole conversation.

Matthew followed up with his principal just to make sure that everything was okay, and he was surprised by what the principal told him: Paszkiewicz had *denied* saying any of the things Matthew mentioned in the letter. Of course, Matthew had evidence contradicting that, so he requested a meeting with both of them, together. After recording eight separate classes, he was ready to play the ace up his sleeve.

Two weeks later, when they met, what could have been a back and forth exchange of accusations and denials turned into more of a courtroom drama. Matthew prepared a list of questions for his teacher, asking whether or not certain comments were made in class. The principal listened as Paszkiewicz denied making some of the comments, suggested that others were misinterpreted, and offered reasons why some of the things he said were perfectly acceptable.

For example, Matthew asked his teacher if he had ever said, "If you reject that, you belong in hell." Paszkiewicz claimed he never said that, adding, "I wouldn't even say that *outside* of the classroom."

Matthew later said of the meeting:

> [Paszkiewicz] portrayed me as an intolerant and ungrateful student who just didn't like the issues he was raising, wasn't open-minded to new information and was trying to ruin his career. He even tried to intimidate me by talking about how he has children and he might lose his job because of me. He also accused me of trying to hurt him on purpose.[5]

That's when Matthew dropped his bombshell by taking a batch of CDs out of his backpack.

There were three sets of two discs, each containing all the lessons Matthew had recorded. Either Paszkiewicz would be vindicated or Matthew's allegations would be proven true. They weren't about to find out. Paszkiewicz requested a union representative before he said any more, and the meeting quickly adjourned. Before he left, though, Paszkiewicz (ignoring his own advice) had a few more words for Matthew:

> To be honest with you, Matt, I'm disappointed because I think that you got the big fish. You're trying to hurt

somebody, maybe you are an atheist, you got the big Christian guy that's a teacher, known and loved for fifteen years and "I brought him down," that's my gut feeling.[6]

His feelings were irrelevant, of course, faced with concrete evidence of his wrongdoing. Matthew's parents, who stood by his side during this whole ordeal, sent letters to the school board and the superintendent demanding they reprimand Paszkiewicz and offer training for teachers so nothing like this would ever happen again.

For weeks, their pleas were ignored. They tried once more, adding that they would go to the press if they didn't hear back. Still no response. Only after a phone call was made to the school board's attorney did they get to speak with a representative from the other side, but it was only to tell Matthew's father that what occurred inside a classroom was none of his business. That was the last straw. It was time to get the media involved.

On November 15, 2006, the *Jersey Journal* ran a picture of Paszkiewicz on its front page with the headline: "Hell Bent." Inside the paper, the actual story ran under a headline quoting Paszkiewicz: "You Belong in Hell." It should have been a clear victory for Matthew.

Instead, the coverage only painted a target on him. The community of Kearny all seemed to take sides, mostly in favor of the popular teacher. Matthew's classmates went on TV to say that Paszkiewicz had done nothing wrong.[7] The superintendent of the district told the press that Paszkiewicz was only leading "high level discussions" in American history, implying that his opinions were not at all out of line. Anonymous commenters on an online bulletin board said that Matthew deserved to be suspended.[8] He received a death threat.[9] He lost friends. Still, the school board and administrators took no public action.

It wasn't until the *New York Times* published its own story on the controversy in mid-December that the school board knew it had to take action; a month later, it finally did. But it wasn't the action Matthew had in mind.

The school board adopted a policy to *ban personal recording devices from the classroom*, unless a student had permission from the teacher and all students were notified.[10]

Needless to say, this only fueled the controversy even more.

At a school board meeting in February, attended by several members of the press, Paszkiewicz told the assembled crowd that he was not guilty of any of the accusations being made against him and that he had been "set up" in the meeting with the principal and Matthew. When it was Matthew's turn to speak, he criticized the school board: "During the whole time, I've been harassed and bullied, and you've done nothing to defend me; you make it look like I've done something wrong."[11]

Matthew had a surprise for them, too. As it turned out, he had also recorded the principal's meeting that Paszkiewicz was referring to.

Faced with the additional piece of audio incrimination and the threat of a lawsuit, the school board finally settled the case with Matthew's family.

The Anti-Defamation League later provided training for the teachers on church/state separation so that this sort of incident would never happen again, and speakers were brought in to Kearny High School to educate students about their rights and what science actually teaches regarding topics like evolution.[12]

Mr. Paszkiewicz kept his job.

When speaking to an audience at the Freedom From Religion Foundation's annual conference a year later, Matthew offered some words of advice for other students who find themselves in a similar situation:

> ... Do not be afraid. When you have the truth, you can prevail as long as you can take the heat. I took the heat, and it has made me a better person... Be careful, be smart, but don't back down. Do what is right. If you have chosen wisely and maintain your

integrity, the consequences will take care of themselves.[13]

This Problem Can Be Fixed

There are many lessons we can take away from this story: Not all teachers and administrators tell the truth; don't lay all your cards on the table at the start of the game; the media can be your friend; document everything.

I would argue, though, that the most important lesson is this one: *Take action.*

Matthew knew that what was happening in his classroom wasn't right, and he did something about it. In so many instances, Christian groups and individuals are able to push religion into public schools because they know no one will ever complain about it—and they're right. We need more students willing to speak up—or, at the very least, raise questions—when they see any sort of religious violation.

What if you're not sure something is wrong? For example, many high schools hold Baccalaureate graduation ceremonies that are religious in nature... Is that okay? Well, as long as the ceremony is optional and not run or sponsored by the school itself, it's perfectly fine. But if you think your school is illegally endorsing the religious ceremony in some way—or it's violating the Constitution in another way—there are many groups that will look into the situation for you. The Secular Student Alliance, Freedom From Religion Foundation, Americans United for Separation of Church and State, and the ACLU, just to name a few, are all there to answer your questions, so send them an email if you're unsure about whether your school is doing something wrong.

Atheists, especially, need to be cognizant of what's legal and what's not, because their classmates, teachers, and administrators may not always know (even if they think they do).

When students have that knowledge, they can fight back. Indeed, many students have, and their stories should serve as inspiration for all the young atheists out there who live in communities where school often feels no different from church.

So that leads us to a big question: Outside of starting groups and filing lawsuits, what can individual atheists in high school do to advocate for their identity and stop illegal promotion of religion?

There are many answers, each worthy of further discussion.

Speak Up

In Matthew LaClair's situation, a teacher had been making religious and political comments in the classroom for *over a decade*, but no one ever did anything about it. We don't know why they all kept silent, but it's very likely that some of those students sat uncomfortably in class, *knowing* their teacher's actions were wrong. Maybe they considered telling an adult, but they thought their word would never be believed. Only Matthew had the foresight to obtain evidence.

Andrew Seidel, an attorney with the Freedom From Religion Foundation, wishes more students would contact FFRF when they notice possible violations of their rights in school. If they're worried about becoming a target of scorn by their classmates, Andrew assures them of confidentiality. But without someone willing to pursue the case, FFRF can't do anything about it.

Case in point: back in 2010, a student at Alexandria High School (in Alabama) knew it was wrong when he heard a student-led prayer over the public address system each morning. In order to put a stop to it, he left a voicemail with the district superintendent and alerted the local ACLU.

Knowing that his classmates would react negatively if they discovered what he had done, he requested anonymity and received it. It was due to his actions that the superintendent soon sent out an email to all the schools in the district letting them know that public prayers, even student-led ones, were against the law.[14]

Sometimes, however, that need for anonymity can prevent a legal resolution to the problem. Andrew mentioned one example of an Alabama school district in which the phrase "God gives meaning and purpose to life" appears directly on the main website. In the same district, the superintendent is known to pray at board meetings and there are prayers at athletics events. All of these things are illegal. A faculty member in the district as well as a student told FFRF about the violations, on separate occasions. However, neither of them wanted to be involved in a potential lawsuit out of fear of being discovered. And without the threat of a lawsuit, the school refused to change its ways, even after a complaint letter was sent.[15]

To be fair, while many of the examples in this book make it sound like all administrators are against atheists, I want to make it very clear that's not the case at all.

One of my blog readers, Andrew, shared a story with me about an incident that took place in his high school back in 2002. In short, he had a substitute teacher in band class who began preaching the Gospel. When the bell rang, he went to the main office and spoke to an assistant principal:

> I gave her a quick rundown of the situation. Her eyes widened when she heard that he was preaching and she said, "That's not right. I'll take care of this," and marched out of the office and down to the band room.

> I went to school in a small town in Indiana where religion is generally considered as American as baseball and apple pie, but the assistant principal knew what the law was and reacted as soon as I let her know what was going on with a minimum [amount] of fuss. I thought my story might be heartening given some of the horror stories that I've seen high school students endure. People shouldn't be afraid of speaking out when they see

this sort of thing, and they might even be
pleasantly surprised at the response they get.[16]

Many students get to know their teachers and counselors
well over the course of their high school careers—but they don't
make an effort to get to know their administrators. That
outreach, from both sides, could do wonders to remedy these
kinds of situations.

Keep in mind that not every objection has to lead to a
legal challenge. In 2007, Dawn Sherman was one of the ten
freshman members of the student council at Buffalo Grove High
School in the northwest suburbs of Chicago. Tasked with
selecting the music for the Homecoming Dance, Dawn saw that
"God Bless America" was on the playlist and suggested it be
removed. "The songs should be secular," she said. That was all it
took. Her fellow council-members agreed to the change.[17]

That simple act may have given her the confidence to
pursue even bigger targets. Later that year, Dawn filed a lawsuit
(with the help of her activist father) to stop a mandatory
moment of silence law that had just been passed in Illinois.
While ultimately unsuccessful, that's the sort of activism and
consciousness-raising that makes a difference and that we
should encourage.

Come Out as an Atheist

If you're an atheist, the most important thing you can
possibly do is *come out of the closet* and let people know you
don't believe in god. A 2011 paper by psychologist Will M.
Gervais showed that as the number of atheists (perceived or
actual) went up, prejudice against atheists went down:[18]

Like atheism, homosexuality is concealable, and
people may similarly be uncertain of how
numerous atheists and homosexuals actually are.
This similarity is strongly emphasized by
[Richard] Dawkins... who argues that anti-atheist

prejudice might be overcome if atheists can find a way to "come out" and raise public awareness of atheism like the Gay Pride movement mobilized widespread support for the acceptance of homosexuality. These movements make plain how numerous atheists and homosexuals actually are.[19]

Obviously, if your parents are forcing you to go to church each week or you risk losing your entire social network, I'm not suggesting you need to come out. But for the many young atheists out there who have the ability to do so, *it is vital that you let people know you're an atheist when opportunities present themselves.* As the saying goes, it's better to be hated for who you are than loved for who you aren't.

Krystal Myers took the opportunity to tell others she was an atheist when she was a student at Tennessee's Lenior City High School. An honors pupil and captain of the swim team, she was a model student. She was also fully aware that her school was illegally promoting religion and discriminating against atheists.

In 2012, as a senior, she wrote an editorial for her school newspaper called "No Rights: The Life of an Atheist" in which she highlighted several examples of those violations: Sectarian prayers at graduation, sectarian prayers at school board meetings, public prayers over the loudspeakers at home football games, a teacher who wore clothing featuring religious symbols, a teacher who encouraged a student to join a religious club, a teacher who wrote Bible quotations on her board.

Krystal noted that atheists like her needed the help of religious students in fighting against these injustices. Unfortunately, school authorities would not let her article run in the paper because of its "potential for disruption."[20]

Ultimately, Krystal was vindicated when the *Knoxville News Sentinel* ran her editorial instead, allowing it to be read by a much wider audience.[21]

You don't always need to stir up controversy to be published. It can often be as easy as just requesting the space.

The *Contra Costa Times* newspaper in California gives local teenagers the chance to contribute opinion pieces and, in 2007, high school senior Suzanne Millward took the opportunity and wrote about why she was an atheist.[22] How many other hyperlocal newspapers would be thrilled to publish free, well-written content by high school students in the area? And if you have that chance, why not use the opportunity to talk about the importance of critical thinking or being an atheist?

Even better than writing an article yourself is having an article written about you. Daniel, the leader of a new Secular Student Alliance high school group in Florida, knew a student who worked on his school's newspaper staff. He pitched her the idea of writing about his new club and she took him up on it. Daniel told me the article had an additional benefit: "It was a chance for us to tell the school who we were, rather than letting them jump to their own conclusions."[23]

As a former editor of my high school newspaper, I remember constantly being on the lookout for a good story, one that my peers would be discussing when the paper came out each month. And nothing gets students talking like a story about atheists meeting after school or an opinion column told from an atheist's perspective.

There's also another important benefit to coming out to your friends: It changes people's perceptions of what they *think* atheists are like. As the Secular Student Alliance's former high school specialist JT Eberhard told me, "It would show people that they don't just *know* atheists; they *like* atheists."[24]

Victory, in any form, for religious conservatives comes at the expense of atheist apathy. If we don't come out, loudly and proudly, we are conceding ground to them. It doesn't always have to be a big production. It can be as simple as changing your "Religious Views" status on Facebook to "atheist." Don't miss out on simple, non-confrontational ways to tell your friends what you think. Even if you're not ready or able to tell people close to you that you don't believe in God, find a way to come out online, even anonymously. For example, you can use a throwaway account on Reddit to explore and comment on its /r/atheism forms. By doing this, you might find that it's easier to come out later in your life without the cloak of anonymity.

Challenge the System

In 2007, Boulder High School (Colorado) senior Emma Martens was frustrated that the Pledge of Allegiance was going to be broadcast on the school's intercom every day. Before then, the Pledge was said in the auditorium before school started and it was voluntary. Emma didn't believe that America was "one nation under God" and she wanted to protest the wording.

She wrote a letter to the principal requesting that the Pledge be moved back to the auditorium at the start of lunch periods, making it optional for anyone who wanted to recite it, but the principal didn't even respond to the letter.

That's what led her to start a protest. As president of Student Worker, an activist club on campus, she knew how to rally students together. The plan was to spend the first few minutes of second period, when the Pledge was going to be recited, in the school's courtyard. On the first day of the Pledge walkout, *nearly one hundred students joined her*. In subsequent weeks, the numbers still remained in the dozens.

While in the courtyard, the students recited an alternative Pledge instead:

> We pledge allegiance to the flag, and our constitutional rights with which it comes, and to the diversity in which our nation stands, one nation part of one planet, with liberty, freedom, choice, and justice for all.

No disciplinary action was taken against the students.[25]

JT Eberhard believes that taking a stand against the Pledge of Allegiance (by protesting or remaining seated) is a fantastic way to both display one's atheism and take a stand against an unnecessary tradition:

No students should have to recite something they don't believe in. If you're going to be kicked out of your house for staying seated during the Pledge, I wouldn't suggest it, but if you're passionate about your non-belief and you want to change society for the other atheists who may be in your class, do it. You will be making a difference and maybe even helping others become more comfortable about their own doubts.[26]

(As a teacher, I think it's worth noting that I can't exactly lead a walkout when the Pledge is said over our school's intercom system. But I can make sure that my students know they are welcome to remain seated during the Pledge if they so desire.)

Alert the Media

Journalists love stories. Good stories have conflict. And the very *idea* of a high school atheist group is rife with conflict in every direction. Can't get a group started? Running a fundraiser for a local charity? Having a joint discussion with members of a religious club? Let members of your local media know!

It sounds like an exaggeration when I write this, but I've found it to be very accurate (if only anecdotally): When atheists do just about *anything*, reporters pay attention. They *want* to write about young atheists. And if there's an actual conflict at play, it makes for an even better story. Furthermore, the media often has the ability to make things right when everyone else seems powerless against the authorities.

Take Brian Lisco, for example. In 2010, as a senior at Stephen F Austin High School in Sugarland, Texas (not far from Houston), Brian attempted to start a Secular Student Alliance group. For months, he kept running into administrative hurdles—like when his principal told him she would authorize the club... but only if Brian changed its name to the Philosophy Club and didn't affiliate with the SSA. To his credit, Brian refused to acquiesce:

We atheists are already invisible—we don't come out. That's a form of repression in itself. It's about getting pushed to the margin of our community.[27]

Still, his club was still not granted official recognition. This also raises the question of whether a religious group—say, the Fellowship of Christian Athletes—would ever be forced to change its name to the "Tim Tebow Fan Club" in order to gain approval.

On two separate occasions, staffers from the Secular Student Alliance emailed the principal to get her to change her mind, but neither got a response back.[28] A phone call with the district's superintendent didn't lead to the club's approval, either.

So what finally got Brian's administration to change its mind?

The Secular Student Alliance contacted *USA Today* religion writer Cathy Lynn Grossman. In February of 2011, Grossman emailed the administrators requesting a comment on why they weren't granting Brian the club.[29] After sending them emails for four straight days—with no response—the principal finally responded to the fifth email with a single line: "He can have his club."[30]

This is the power of the media. And it also suggests something a bit more perverse: That the school administrators who stop these clubs from forming *know* that what they're doing is wrong; they just don't want the public to find out about it. But shine a local or national spotlight on their malfeasance and they'll cave.

Get Educated

Obviously, all students should work hard in their academic classes, but I'd also encourage young atheists to learn about atheism. Even though it's technically one answer ("No") to one question ("Does God exist?"), so much more has been written about the subject and it's important to understand the kinds of discussions atheists tend to have outside of a classroom setting.

Read books and watch lectures by popular Christian apologists so you know the kinds of arguments they make when trying to prove God's existence. (Writers Lee Strobel and Josh McDowell offer particularly low-hanging fruit.) You should also read books and watch lectures by atheists so you know how they rebut what the other side says. In hundreds of years, very little has changed in the way Christians defend their faith and how atheists refute it. There are no new ideas; only new ways of presenting them. At the end of this book, I offer my own suggestions of the best resources you can use to educate yourselves on the subject, but I want to make it clear that there is no shortage of excellent books, videos, blogs, etc. You just have to start browsing.

Go through a library or bookstore's religion section and start reading books about the subject. Listen to atheist podcasts, watch atheists on YouTube, and read atheist bloggers to learn about current events from a non-religious perspective. It will help you understand and interpret news stories. Unlike the books by the "New Atheists," which offer more general arguments against religion, the atheists on the Internet are able to tackle much more specific issues in addition to the general ones. If something happens in the news, you will likely hear an atheist's perspective on it before long.

Learn about your rights. You don't have to be a future lawyer to understand that you have a right to be an outspoken atheist at your school, that you have the right to form an atheist student group (provided there are other non-curricular groups at your school), that you have the right to remain seated during the Pledge of Allegiance, and that you have the right to a public school education where one faith isn't promoted over another and theism isn't promoted over atheism.

Learn about your classmates: What do they believe? Why do they believe it? Very few classes offer students the chance to debate their views in an educational context, so having conversations about religion with your friends outside of school can lead to fascinating revelations. (Have you ever asked Christian friends if they think Anne Frank is in Hell? Try it. It's fun.)

And just to bring it back to the classroom, there's plenty you can do *in school* to express your identity and prepare yourself for the future.

- If you are assigned to write an open-ended essay, talk about your atheism (if appropriate).

- Learn about evolution in your science classes so that you can defend science against Creationists and Intelligent Design proponents.

- Learn about how religion has played a role in shaping world history (for better and for worse).

- Read banned books. There are a lot of religious groups that don't want you to have access to certain books because they contain "immoral" or "indecent" content. Fight back. And don't just read those books; pass them along to your friends.

- And then learn about imaginary numbers in math class. Because, like all gods, even if they're not real, there's plenty to be said about them.

Share Your Ideas

It takes a lot of motivation to start a journal or blog when you're not sure anyone's ever going to read it, but getting your thoughts about religion (or anything, really) in writing is a wonderful way to document your own growth and share your thoughts with the world. I would encourage you to write in a way that's public only because you never know who might connect with what you're saying. It's a humbling and uplifting experience when you realize your own experience is almost identical to someone else's. I've found through my own blogging that many atheists have gone through the same things as I did when leaving my parents' faith. When you're able to bounce your ideas off of other atheists, you can refine and clarify your views. That will make it much easier to deal with disapproving parents, religious people you might date, and even other family members at weddings or funerals taking place in a church.

If that's too much, consider something simpler: Share your opinions on Twitter. Update your status on Facebook with your thoughts on current events. Post a meme reflecting your views on a Tumblr page. It doesn't matter. It doesn't even have to be about religion. The point is to share your ideas and thoughts with other people and become comfortable with doing that.

If you're part of a student group and you do something you're proud of—say you run a successful blood drive, raise money for charity, volunteer with one of the religious groups at your school—tell the Secular Student Alliance (or your favorite blogger, hint hint) so they can share what you did with other groups.

A Positive Path Forward

Atheists have always been a part of the student body, but they're embracing their secular identities in a way we've never seen before. In part, that means they're watchdogs in their own schools, alerting the world to instances of religious encroachment. But it also means they're playing offense as well as defense. It's not enough to fight back every time religious battles arise; we need young atheists to also promote their beliefs in positive ways. If you're looking for ways to do that, the next chapter offers all sorts of ideas.

7

Curriculum

Ways to Spread Friendly Atheism

Here's a question every atheist group leader has heard at some point: "What do atheists do when they meet? Do they just sit around and not pray?" (Cue no laughter.)

Any good extra-curricular activity gives students an opportunity to express themselves and learn skills they can carry with them into the future. Atheist groups are no different. Yet, at any given public school, you're far more likely to run across a religious group than an atheist one. Besides the stigma attached to the word "atheist," and the suspicion that other students would not join such a club, it's possible that one of the reasons these groups don't always begin is because students aren't sure what they would do during meetings.

In fact, there are lots of activities high school atheist groups can do that will educate students, help their communities, and promote civil dialogue. This is by no means meant to be an exhaustive list; these are merely suggestions for what groups can do (and have done) for their members.

Have a Religion Roundtable

Students can give a presentation to the group about the beliefs they were raised with: what they believed, why they believed it, and what ultimately led them to stop believing it. If the majority of students share the same religious background, consider doing research on a different religion and sharing those findings with the group. This isn't about making fun of those religions; it's about educating each other on various belief systems and realizing that people accept all sorts of unsupported ideas because of what a holy book or ancient figure once said.

Host Debates

Partner with a religious group at your school and host a debate for any students who want to attend. It could be generic (debating the existence of God) or specific (debating whether or not we should teach Creationism in the classroom), formal or informal. One added benefit to this is that you avoid a boring conversation where everyone just agrees with each other. One student I spoke with told me that he makes sure he's on good terms with his school's Prayer Group: "At first, they were planning on 'infiltrating the SSA to spread the Bible,' but now we're talking about meeting together occasionally and even [hosting] structured debates."[1] If working with another group on campus isn't a possibility, consider debating differences of opinions within your group (e.g., Is atheism a religion? Are atheists truly discriminated against in our society?).

Write

Spend a meeting writing letters-to-the editor of your local or campus newspaper about issues with which group members disagree.[2] This is one of those tasks that seem daunting at first but the payoff of getting published is well worth it.

Similarly, consider starting a group blog and having members contribute to it—getting people comfortable with talking about their religious doubts (and dealing with the responses to their posts) is a great way to prepare them for future conversations.

Discuss Books

Even though it's tough to get students to read an entire book on top of the mountain of homework they already have, it may be a little easier to discuss a chapter of a book. Or a blog post. Or an essay. Better yet, consider discussing a chapter of a religious book (someone's bound to have a copy of *The Case for Christ*...) and talking about why the arguments in it are faulty.

Have an Atheist Bible Study

This may be even better than a book club. Read Bible chapters and discuss them. The passages may be short but the implications are huge. This is more beneficial if there's a former or current Christian in the group who may have more contextual knowledge of the verses or has the experience of hearing a sermon in which the verses in question were discussed. If most students are already well-versed in the Bible, try studying the Quran or the Book of Mormon.

Help Other Minority Reports

Atheists tend to know what it's like to be an unaccepted minority in a high school. So show support for other minorities at the school. At Rutherford High School in Florida, the Secular Student Alliance took part in a chalking campaign in support of LGBT students, writing messages like "Gay is OK" on the sidewalk. Their principal approved the activity because it went "hand in hand with [the school's] anti-bullying campaign."[3]

Stick Together

As we've seen in case after case, young atheists often feel alone in their thinking, and when they challenge religion in their public school, they're left to fend for themselves. It's an inside joke in the secular community that bringing together atheists is like herding cats. However, a secular student group at a school can provide a built-in support system for atheists who want to come out to their families, sit down during the Pledge, or file a lawsuit against their district in the case of improper religious intrusion.

Perform Community Service

Most high schools require a set number of community service hours to be completed in order for students to graduate. Use that as a starting point to find out where help is needed in your community and have your atheist group members volunteer. Don't just meet the minimum number of service hours; exceed it by a long shot. This would show the community that local atheists care about their neighborhoods and display the kind of caring morality that many Christians doubt exists in non-believers.

Raise Money for Good Causes

In the event of a natural disaster like Hurricane Katrina or the earthquake in Haiti, student groups are usually allowed to collect change from students in classrooms or the cafeteria. That money can be given to the Red Cross or another worthy secular organization. (Just be sure to get approval from your administrators first.) Within your own group, consider hosting a Flying Spaghetti Monster Pasta Party to raise the money, too.

Be Proud

Okay, this isn't an activity so much as a mindset. Young people who question their faith often feel like there's something wrong with them. They worry that God is testing them or that they're punching themselves a one-way ticket to Hell. An atheist group can give them the confidence to know there's nothing wrong with them and that they are part of a tradition of radical questioning that has gone on for millennia.

Host a Panel Discussion about Dealing with Parents

Imagine a few students at a table: one who still hasn't told her parents she's an atheist, one who did but faced consequences for it, one who did and everything turned out okay. Also there is a religious parent who has an atheist child. What a terrific opportunity to ask questions and get advice. Invite your guidance counselor to participate, too.

Watch Movies

There are many documentaries and feature films dealing with the topic of religion. *Saved, Inherit the Wind*, Julia Sweeney's *Letting Go of God*, and *Jesus Camp* work wonders as conversation-starters. So do episodes of TV shows like *Mythbusters* and Carl Sagan's *Cosmos*. A longer list of TV/movie suggestions can be found at http://www.secularstudents.org/movies.

It's also a chance to relax and have fun with other members of your group, as you share food and drinks while being entertained. Invite other students to join you. If possible, hold a discussion about the movie immediately afterward, so that there's a forum for students' questions and concerns. (Depending on the movie's rating, students may need a signed permission slip from parents. Check with your faculty sponsor in that case.)

Run for Office

Whenever there's a student body election taking place at your school, make sure someone from your group is running for leadership positions. If other group members support that candidate, have them manage the campaign. In addition to having a voice of reason in a position of power, it will both encourage students to run for public office in the future and teach students how to help get a candidate elected. No doubt we could use more atheists in both roles once they graduate.

Ask an Atheist

The Secular Student Alliance holds a national Ask An Atheist Day on the third Thursday in April each year.[4] This is a chance for groups to set up a booth in a public location so that other students can stop by, ask questions, and have a civil, respectful dialogue with the atheist students. It's also a chance to defeat the stereotypes about atheism by presenting welcoming faces to those with questions.

Encourage Good Citizenship

While colleges may be better venues for hosting voter registration drives, high school students can encourage students in Driver's Education classes to sign up as organ donors. (In the state of Illinois, where I'm from, sixteen-year-olds can make that decision when they get their licenses.) With the permission of the teachers, atheist group members could make a completely secular case for why all students ought to become donors in front of their classmates.

Host a Speaker

There may be local activists, religious and non-religious leaders, or politicians in your area who would be happy to share their stories with students after school for no cost. The Secular Student Alliance and CFI On Campus can provide grant money if an honorarium is needed. The best way to learn how to be an activist/leader is to hear from one first-hand, so invite some to your school. Host those discussions—better yet, do it in conjunction with a religious group—and allow time for a question-and-answer session afterward.

Be Aware of Local/State Politics

Many pieces of pro-religious legislation pass through state legislatures without argument because many citizens are simply unaware of what is happening. It happens even more at local levels, where city councils are often prone to include Christian prayers before the start of meetings. Similarly, school boards can pass curriculum changes instantly if people aren't there to raise objections. That means group members should be alert when it comes to local/state news and upcoming legislation. Read the newspaper and follow state government websites. If necessary, attend those meetings, speak out against bad legislation, and *get it all on video* so the rest of us can learn from your example.

The Benefit for Religious Students

It should be noted that just about all of these activities are not limited to atheists only. Religious students may also enjoy the conversations that take place when surrounded by atheists.

When I began an atheist group at my college in Chicago, I remember two students from a local Christian school who often attended our weekly discussions. They were quick to challenge us if we said anything untrue about their faith and they were always willing to raise questions we weren't asking. When we asked them why they came to our meetings, their answer was unexpected. They said they just never had these kinds of conversations at their school; they were expected to accept what they were told and not to question their faith. But our atheist group, while not changing their minds about Christianity, challenged them in a way their own school did not and we gave them a lot to think about. We were all better off because of their contributions to our discussions.

While all of the activities above are geared toward atheist students, they also provide an educational experience for religious students who are not used to being around openly atheistic people. In addition to benefitting the school as a whole, these groups help students obtain a stronger sense of self and community; they also offer some long-term benefits to young atheists that aren't always evident as the events are happening. They may be even more important for their development as they graduate and head out into the "real world."

Most of these suggestions can be started and completed within the course of a single meeting. They're short-term activities for your group designed to foster a positive and safe atmosphere for secular students. But they also help achieve some long-term benefits that we also have to consider for these groups.

Creating a Sense of Community Beyond High School

When students get involved with a club in school, they learn the basics of creating and leading a group, skills that will help them in college and after they graduate. They will hopefully see the value of gathering with other atheists, discussing topics relevant to their interests, and taking action on issues that treat Secular Americans as second-class citizens.

Retaining Your Secular Identity As You Grow Older

There used to be a time when I would attend atheist conferences and see large contingents of college-aged students and senior citizens... and barely anyone in-between. The reason was that as people began their careers and started families, there was little time or reason for them to be thinking about atheism-related topics. When they got married, had children, or wanted to do any volunteer work, the church was the place to go.

Now, however, there are resources available for people who want secular alternatives to religious ceremonies. You can now have a non-religious wedding, teach children ethics and morals without a religious framework, and do good in your area without the help of a faith-based group. By being part of a non-religious community or just embracing that part of your identity from a young age, you can learn how to celebrate important events in your life without resorting to religion to mark the occasion.

Teaching Critical Thinking Skills

This is something one would hope students learn to do in their classes, but atheist groups are especially adept at getting students to examine some of their most cherished beliefs, to question authority when its warranted, and to demand evidence when someone makes an unrealistic claim. Those are not always skills taught in academic classes, but they are undoubtedly useful later in life.

Exposing Students to New Career Options

For years, it was not possible to be a "professional atheist." That's no longer the case. With dozens of organizations representing tens of thousands of atheist members nationwide, there are now job opportunities for students who want to become full-time activists after they graduate from college. Many of these jobs didn't exist a decade ago.

Andrew Seidel, whom I've mentioned earlier in this book, is one of the four full-time staff attorneys for the Freedom From Religion Foundation. He feels lucky to be fighting for this cause: "I have no doubt that what I am doing is right. That's not always the case in law, much of the time. As a lawyer, arguing these cases for FFRF, there's no compromising your values." Andrew told me he relishes the challenges he faces, including helping families fight school administrators that push religion into the schools. Even though it's possible he could be making much more money at a private law firm, he loves his job and knows that his work has a genuinely positive impact on the world:

> I am in love with the Constitution. Every day, I am fighting to uphold that document and the principles underlying it, and there are so few lawyers who get the opportunity to do that. To me, that is the greatest thing about this line of work.[5]

Deeply devout Christians can go through school knowing there will always be an opportunity to get a job promoting their faith after they graduate, whether it means becoming a youth pastor, getting a staff position for an organization like Cru (formerly Campus Crusade for Christ), or working at a Christian school. These may not be high-paying jobs, but they are career options. Now, young atheists are starting to see jobs that, like Andrew's, put to use their education, passion, and activism.

Break the Stereotypes and Take Action

Again, all of this is just a glimpse of the benefits one can get by either being part of a secular student group or just openly identifying as an atheist from a young age. There are drawbacks, too, as we've seen, but I would argue the benefits outweigh any of the potential pitfalls.

I would also add that students who do any of these things should do them with a smile on their faces and with a calm, gentle demeanor. When the stereotype of an "angry atheist" is so prevalent, it's important not to give people any reason to think that's true. That's not to say we can't be angry on the inside, but it's to our benefit not to lash out against religious people publicly when a more composed statement serves the same purpose. Especially at a high school or college, it would be counterproductive to turn people away from atheism because of how we act in the same way fire-and-brimstone preachers turn people away from Christianity. Break the stereotypes. It's eye-opening for others and it will help you out in the long run.

It has never been more important—and easier—to talk about your beliefs in high school. You can do it on your own, but if you're looking to start a group, all you have to do is request a Group Starting Packet from the Secular Student Alliance.[6]

We need more students with the courage and leadership skills to get these groups off the ground at their own schools. We need more students who can inspire their peers to be open about their religious doubts. We need students with the knowledge of how to run a successful group and pass the reins to a new generation of student leaders when they go off to college. These students are out there, but we need to give them to tools to flourish.

So is there anything the rest of us do to help them out? Absolutely. Students shouldn't have to figure all this out on their own. In fact, parents, teachers, administrators, and religious allies all have a vital role to play in the development of young atheists.

8

The PTA

How Parents, Teachers, and Administrators Can Help Young Atheists

Though many of the students I've profiled up to this point had to struggle just to get their schools to follow the law, perhaps nobody had it as bad as Michael Chandler. Michael was in a district where violations of church-state separation weren't just occasional occurrences; they were literally a part of the schedule.

What makes his story especially interesting is that Michael wasn't a student at the school. He was one of the administrators.

For twenty-five years, he worked in the DeKalb County School District in Stone Mountain, Georgia, just northeast of Atlanta. He spent the first twelve years as a teacher before being appointed as assistant principal of Valley Head High School (actually a K-12 school) in 1985. One of his first tasks, assigned to him by the principal, was to schedule a time for the Ponderosa Bible Camp to come into the classrooms and teach Bible lessons.

Even though Michael pointed out the potential legal issues to his boss, he was told this was a tradition and it would continue, so Michael did as he was told. This was a new job, after all, and he didn't want to seem too pushy. Every month for the rest of the school year, a portion of academic time was set aside for religious indoctrination at the hands of the Christian group. Students who wished to be excused had the option of sitting in the hallway or going to the principal's office. No matter which option students chose—if they chose one at all—the other students were bound to "criticize, ostracize, and demonize" them.[1]

Michael didn't realize how bad things were for kids who chose not to participate until he sat down with two new transfer students:

> One day during my second year at Valley Head I was enrolling two little girls in school. They were in third or fourth grade. These two girls came from another school in the same system so they were aware of how things worked in DeKalb County. I finished and I asked them if they had any questions. One girl looked at me and asked, "Do you have Bible stories in this school?"
>
> I said, "I'm afraid we do. Why do you ask?"
>
> Tears ran from that little girl's big brown eyes. She teared up and said, "At my other school I had to sit in the hall and the kids were mean to me."
>
> That was a number of years ago, but I can still see that little girl's face today. She was harassed and intimidated because she was, at that point, a Jehovah's Witness, and her mom didn't want her listening to the Bible stories.
>
> I looked in her eyes and decided that day... to do something, or do what I could, to stop it.[2]

He surveyed the teachers who had to cut class short to make room for the monthly Bible lessons and discovered that several of them felt as he did—that religious proselytizing had no place in a public school. Michael took that information to his principal and a change was made: There would be no more Bible lessons for students in grades four through six. However, the principal said, students from kindergarten through third grade would continue them because they "need their Bible stories."[3]

It wasn't good enough. Michael took his complaint to the district superintendent and, with his reputation on the line, got the district to stop the Bible lessons completely. It was a victory, but it fixed only one of many infractions in the district. Michael wasn't done yet.

The Gideons—best known for putting Bibles in hotel rooms—were his next opponents. As you might expect, their goal was to get a copy of the Bible into as many hands as possible, including those of schoolchildren. For years, well-dressed representatives came to Valley Head, visiting the fifth through eleventh grade classrooms, handing copies of the New Testament to the children. If any student refused, the Gideons rep would say, "Why not? You need this. It will save your soul. You need to take this home to your mother and father."[4]

Michael, again, spoke with his principal about the legal problems surrounding bringing religion into the classroom and, again, it worked. The Gideons were banished from the classrooms. But they didn't disappear entirely. Instead, they set up shop at a sidewalk across the street from the school, hoping to catch students as they left the building. Just to avoid the Bible-thumpers, Michael made sure the buses for the youngest children were rerouted to pick them up from the back of the building.

The arms race didn't stop there. One day, when the Gideons knew Michael would be out of the office, they went directly onto the buses to give the Bibles to children. "Even Alabama says you can't do that," Michael said later.

On another occasion the following fall, on a day warm enough that the windows on the buses were down, the Gideons *threw Bibles through the windows* in order to get them in the hands of students. Michael only found out what happened because he ran into a student the next day who had a cut lip as a result of being hit by one of the books.

The Gideons kept at it for several years. When Michael's own son Jesse began fifth grade—the first grade level the

Gideons paid special attention to—he came home with a New Testament. When pressed, Jesse said that he took it because he "thought he had to." Michael couldn't believe it:

> The separation of church and state failed because the school gave him the impression [that accepting the Bible] was something he was supposed to do— it had the school stamp of approval on it.[5]

It resulted in another argument with the principal, who told Michael, *"You're going to hell* because you dare question what I'm doing."

It was 1994. Michael had been in his administrative position for nine years.

At that point, he began reaching out to attorneys who could help him file a lawsuit against the district. Of the twenty-five or so lawyers he contacted in the state of Alabama, not a single one accepted the case. It would hurt business too much to side with someone trying to get religion out of the classroom. Finally, he spoke with the ACLU. Its representatives told Michael to document everything, which he did for the next two years, videotaping instances of Christianity permeating into the public school curriculum and getting his colleagues to do the same.

After all that time, what did Michael find?

- The D.A.R.E. drug-awareness program, mandatory for fifth graders, included a Bible reading and minister-led devotional.[6] (The teacher in charge curiously argued that the Bible verses weren't "religious in nature.")

- Local ministers at a Parent Teacher Organization meeting delivered two separate invocations.

- Jesse's fifth-grade teacher made sure a Bible story was read aloud before the kids went to lunch.

- Homeroom teachers would pass out flyers advertising church events.

- Devotionals were recited over the loudspeakers before home football games, which Michael was required to attend as an administrator.

- Graduation services and mandatory school assemblies included prayers or Bible readings.

On February 1, 1996, Michael finally filed his lawsuit against the district with the help of Americans United for Separation of Church and State and the ACLU. Even though the county's attorney signed paperwork promising all religious activities would stop, they didn't.

A member of the school board later referenced the lawsuit by saying that the majority ought to rule in cases like this and anybody who didn't like it could go "return to wherever they came from."

Michael wasn't sure how to take that:

> I've lived here for forty-seven years. I have nowhere to go. So he's going to have to put up with me for a lot longer.[7]

The lowest point during the Chandler family's fight may have been that following October, when young Jesse went to eat lunch. By this time, students were aware that his father was trying to "ban Christianity" from the schools. As Jesse stepped into the cafeteria that day—and many others after that—nearly two hundred other students stood up to recite the Lord's Prayer. This was hardly free exercise of religion; it was bullying. It was a verbal slap in the face to Jesse's entire family. When Michael heard about the incident, he asked his son if everything was okay and if there was anything he could do. Jesse responded courageously:

I'm all right. As long as it doesn't bother me, they're not winning.[8]

Eventually, though, Jesse began to eat lunch in a separate classroom instead of going back into the cafeteria.

Michael, who also held teaching duties at his school, wasn't immune from the Christian students' retaliation. According to one of his students, "When he comes into the class, we stop whatever we're doing and start talking loudly about the Bible."[9]

Those students would have been surprised to learn that Michael was a Christian, too.[10] He just believed in the separation of church and state.

Judge Ira DeMent finally told the school in March of 1997 to put a stop to all religious activities immediately. He reaffirmed that ruling later in the year.[11] In his judgment, Judge DeMent delineated what the law did and didn't allow.[12]

What did it allow? Students could use religious textbooks in an objective way. They could pray or proselytize on their own time (not during class). They could make a reference to God in a speech as long as it didn't call for an audience response. They could announce meetings of religious clubs over the intercom. They could wear jewelry or clothing expressing their faith (appropriately).

What students and teachers were *not* allowed to do was lead prayers during class time, graduation ceremonies, or over the intercom. They could not allow third parties (like the Gideons) to hand out Bibles on their property or during class time.

Despite the ruling permitting private prayer and limited public acknowledgment of God, Christians were incensed. Dean Young, the head of the state's Christian Family Association, believed the Constitution needed to take a backseat to his faith:

> It is a sad day in this state and nation when a single judge can force his opinion on the people of Alabama when the vast majority of the citizens in

this state disagree with that opinion... If one federal judge can dictate to the people of this state how they cannot perform religious activities, we are not very far from the time when they will remove all religious rights of the people.[13]

Of course, the only activities that were banned were the ones that suggested school endorsement of religion or forced that religion upon students against their wishes.

While the Eleventh Circuit Court of Appeals rejected part of Judge DeMent's ruling (thus *allowing* student-led prayers at graduation and over the intercom system),[14] the Supreme Court later vacated that ruling in 2000 in *Chandler v. Siegelman*,[15] forcing the Appeals court to reconsider its decision.[16]

It took well over a decade, but Michael ultimately prevailed.

What Good Faculty Sponsors Do

When you hear about young atheists who struggle in their high schools, it's tempting to blame the schools' administrators since they are so often responsible for blocking a group's formation or letting religious privilege go unchecked. However, Michael Chandler is one of the many good administrators out there, working to protect *all* students instead of just the majority of them.

But why don't we hear about more of them? Why does Michael seem to be an exception rather than the norm? Shouldn't administrators, regardless of their personal beliefs, be following the law and helping *all* students explore their religious identities in a legal, inclusive way?

They should. The Secular Student Alliance makes the point succinctly:

Teachers, school officials and administrators bear a legal and moral obligation to safeguard the well-being of nontheistic students. All students are entitled to be treated with respect in a public school environment, regardless of their beliefs.[17]

Like the statement indicates, this begins at the top. We need administrators to be cognizant of the law. When it comes to religion, individual students have a right to practice their beliefs so long as they don't impose them on other students. Adults who work in schools should be made aware of this, especially so religious and non-religious clubs don't face unnecessary obstacles to their formation. That also means they have an obligation to keep Christian groups from pushing their faith *through* the schools, whether by speaking at assemblies or bringing Bibles into the classroom. If faculty and staff members see a potential violation of the law happening in their school or district, their superiors have to be informed about the problem.

That's not easy. I suspect many good teachers and administrators remain silent—like Michael Chandler was for many years—because they don't want their jobs to be in jeopardy for doing the right thing. However, groups like FFRF can send warning letters to the superintendent or principal without "outing" the person who tipped them off. In any case, faculty members can learn an important lesson from Michael: Keep your eyes open and alert and take action on any violations you see. Don't wait for the problem to get resolved on its own. It rarely ever does.

If administrators are looking for a place to start when it comes to educating faculty members on these issues, the "Religious Liberty in Public Schools" section of the First Amendment Center's website offers some fantastic resources.[18]

Outside of reporting legal violations, the most helpful thing staff members can to do help young atheists may be putting themselves out there as non-theistic role models.

If students ask their teachers what church they attend, it's perfectly acceptable for teachers to say they don't attend one at all. If there's a class discussion in English or history and religion comes up, teachers don't have to avoid the topic—they can let students talk about their beliefs while respectfully playing devil's advocate (on all sides) just to show there are alternative points of view when it comes to religious beliefs. If a school librarian asks faculty members to put signs outside their doors letting students know what books they're reading—to show students that the adults in the school read for fun—there's nothing wrong with listing a book written by an atheist.

In fact, Daniel, a student at Wekiva High School in Florida, met his atheist group's eventual faculty sponsor because he noticed what books that teacher was reading:

> When I visited my Psychology teacher-to-be during orientation, I noticed the wonderful *The God Delusion* on his "List of Books that Influenced My Life"... In addition to his atheism, I later found him to have a sort of activist demeanor about him and [he] eagerly accepted my request [to become the group sponsor]. Whatever disagreements there have been, it would be difficult to conceive [of] a better sponsor, and [I] feel immense sympathy for a group without the fortune ours had.[19]

I understand the value of teachers being completely impartial in the classroom. They don't want any religious students to feel uncomfortable in their presence and I'm not suggesting teachers do anything to ruin that relationship with their students. What I am advocating for is that atheist teachers not hide that fact about themselves when the opportunity presents itself. Those teachers may be the only other atheists a student has ever met, and if that student knows that his or her teacher doesn't believe in a god, it makes it easier for the student to accept that, too.

Just to be clear, everything I'm suggesting here is completely legal. I'm not saying teachers should spend class time talking about why God doesn't exist. I'm also not telling teachers to encourage students to begin an atheist group. (Even if those things were legal, I believe they would be bad ideas.) This is simply about teachers not shielding who they are from their students if they inquire about it. Some of the adults I've mentioned in this book—like Matthew LaClair's teacher David Paszkiewicz—crossed the line between teaching and preaching. Atheist teachers shouldn't stoop to their level.

What else can teachers do to help? To begin with, they should seriously consider becoming sponsors for secular student groups if a student asks for their help. Not only would the students overcome one of the toughest hurdles in forming a group, but they would also have an advocate on their side.

Kirk Mefford is one of those faculty members proudly supporting his atheist students. A science teacher at a high school in Madison, Wisconsin, Mefford is a co-advisor to his school's Freedom From Religion Club. On the club's Facebook page, the group's description says, tongue-in-cheek, that its members "have also been called the anti-religion club, the anti-god club, the atheist club, and the join-it-to-make-your-parents-angry club."[20]

Joking aside, Mefford explained the importance of sponsoring such a group this way:

> We do not dwell on how we feel marginalized. We are educated adults, and we are comfortable and confident in our identities. We are not intimidated by people who do not approve of our position on religion. We are concerned with the well-being of the students who question religion and the value society places on religious faith. They are young, often unprepared to hold their ground in a verbal dispute and trained by society to trust and submit to adults. They may even feel physically intimidated by other students and adults, and they seek the approval of adults and the acceptance of their peers. They are the ones most affected by the abuse by Christians.

A great student member left the club this year because his religious friends were offended by his membership in the club. This exemplifies the pressures that many of our student members unfortunately face. We believe that it's especially important to support students who are members of groups that have historically been discriminated against.[21]

Mefford's group has three goals:

- To support students who choose to break away from the religion in which they were indoctrinated.

- To inform students of the dangers of religious dogma.

- To inspire students to accept personal responsibility for making their lives rewarding and meaningful.

How incredible would young atheists' high school experiences be if every school had groups and faculty sponsors like this? And while these groups are all about the students, I have no doubt that the faculty members also get immense satisfaction from the discussions and activities that take place.

Michael Creamer certainly felt that way when he helped students start a Secular Student Alliance at Rutherford High School in Panama City, Florida. Rutherford is a school of approximately 1,400 students, and many of them are religious. For years, when they would ask Mr. Creamer which church he belonged to—a common question for anyone living in the South—he would just avoid the conversation and say he wasn't comfortable discussing that topic with students. But after a while, he realized that Christian teachers *never responded the same way*. They were always willing to talk about their faith and their church. They embraced their religion and felt no need to hide that part of their lives from students.

So why was he so scared of doing the same thing?

> We have to do that, too. There's nothing to be ashamed of. Every time we pull back, [it's like] there's something wrong with being atheist or agnostic.

Eventually, he stopped worrying. The next time a student asked him about his churchgoing, he answered honestly: "My family doesn't attend church. I'm an atheist. My wife is an atheist."

Two things helped soften the blow of this answer: First, Michael had taught at Rutherford for nearly three decades. He had a good reputation: The students loved him and the administrators knew he was a solid teacher. His religious beliefs—whatever they were—weren't going to get in the way of that. Second, he taught students in accelerated classes where candid discussions about philosophy and religion were already part of the courses. One of the classes he taught was called "Theory of Knowledge," a compulsory course for students seeking to earn an International Baccalaureate degree. No conversation about "knowledge" was complete without talking about how scientific progress had advanced throughout history and how the Church had often served as an obstacle to it. Even though Michael approached those discussions in an even-handed way, students were given the chance to discuss the pros and cons of church and their teacher served as a fair moderator for the conversation.

In 2010, students from his class approached him about wanting to start a group for atheists. They figured he might be willing to do it since he was openly atheist himself and the sign on his classroom door read, "Don't believe everything you think."

While he might have shied away from a faculty sponsor role in the past, he wasn't going to ignore the request now.

Michael asked for an announcement about the club to be made over the loudspeakers for atheist and agnostic students to meet in his classroom if they wanted to be a part of this group. The group was popular from the moment it launched, with thirty students attending the first meeting.[22] They met weekly after school, discussing anything from being an atheist in a religious community, to the latest lawsuits regarding church/state separation, to books about atheism that they had read. At the last meeting of each month, the students watched a movie (like Bill Maher's *Religulous*) while scarfing down popcorn and pizza.

Michael estimates that nearly a quarter of the attendees are not "full-blown" atheists or agnostics. They're still developing their views on religion. But this is the one club at the school where doubting and questioning are cherished assets.

At one point in the spring of 2011, the *New York Times* ran an article about the group. It was a positive piece focusing on both Michael ("the Atticus Finch of Rutherford High") and the students attending the meetings. When I read it, though, the final paragraphs were the ones that stuck with me:

> There are students who do not want their parents to know they belong to an atheist club. "I tell my mother I'm at Ocean Club," one girl said.
>
> Another member said her father, who is in the Navy, would be angry and disappointed in her. "He keeps a roof over my head," she said. "I wouldn't want to fight with him." She asked that her name not be used for fear it would hurt her father. "I don't want us to grow apart over this," she said."[23]

The inability of those students to be honest about their beliefs with their parents struck a nerve with me and many other readers, too. Perhaps it was disappointing to realize that, even for a club with a strong faculty sponsor and large membership, not all students could be open about their views on religion.

Despite that, the response to the article was overwhelmingly positive. Michael received numerous emails and phone calls from students and teachers who were also atheists. In addition, readers sent him enough books about atheism—as did some of the books' authors—to nearly fill up his classroom bookshelf, creating a mini-library for students who wanted to borrow the literature. More importantly, the article sent a strong message to the Rutherford group's members: *You're making a difference for other young atheists out there.*

Even today, Michael still has obstacles to overcome. Every year, he says, one or two students drop his classes when they discover he's an atheist. He also has to deal with faculty members who disapprove of the group's existence (though none try to shut it down). But if the students can be courageous enough to come out as atheists, he believes atheist teachers should also have the fortitude to stand up to their colleagues:

> You've got to be able to stand up at the faculty meeting and say, "Hey listen, my Secular Student Alliance did this" knowing 95 percent of people in that room don't want to hear about it. If you're not willing to do that, I don't think it's going to go.[24]

Michael encourages other atheist teachers to be candid about their beliefs in their classroom. Not that they should use their classroom as a personal forum to attack religion, but that they should be honest about who they are. "If the question is asked," he told me, "it needs to be answered. And it needs to be answered forthrightly."

What Supportive Parents Can Do

Even though some of the Rutherford students couldn't tell their parents about their atheism, not all parents are unapproachable. Parents who support their child's non-religious identity can help students and student groups, too.

The most important way to help, depending on where you live, may be to run for the school board.

Just as we saw in Dover, Pennsylvania[25] and Cobb County, Georgia,[26] local boards of education can play a tremendous role in the way proper science is taught to our students. Even history curricula can go astray, as the state of Texas showed us in 2010.[27]

We need parents who are willing to embrace challenging, evidence-based curricula in their kids' districts and who can stand up to members of the Religious Right who are actively trying to win school board elections specifically so they can stop what they see as affronts to their faith, like sex education classes.[28]

Both religious and non-religious parents would also be doing their atheist teenagers a huge favor by simply supporting their decisions to start a group or be activists at their school.

Stu Tanquist tells a story in Dale McGowan's book *Parenting Beyond Belief* that shows how effective that can be:

> While attending eighth-grade parent-teacher conferences, we were informed soberly that our daughter was not standing for the Pledge of Allegiance. I was unaware that she had made this decision and glowed with pride. Having children stand and recite a rote pledge to their country is something I would not expect from a free democratic nation—especially when they are further compelled to declare that nation to be "under God." If our country deserves the respect of its citizens, that respect should be earned and freely and individually expressed...
>
> I asked the teacher why he thought it was important to share this information about our daughter. He began squirming in his seat, then said at last that it really wasn't important—he just thought we would want to know. I reported that it

must be important to him since he felt compelled to bring it up. Again, the same awkward response. He clearly understood that our daughter was within her legal right to abstain, and it was now painfully apparent that I was unsympathetic to his concern. Recognizing that this issue was now a non-issue, I moved on to talk about things that really mattered, like our daughter's academic progress and learning needs.[29]

What Local Atheist Groups Can Do

Finally, local atheist groups also have a role to play in the development of high school students. This is a little trickier because the members of these groups don't necessarily have a direct connection to the students, but they can still provide important resources to them.

For example, since many groups do local service projects, they can let high school guidance counselors know when opportunities come up for students to join them. Many high schools require students to complete a certain number of community service hours in order to graduate—and churches are more than happy to provide those opportunities for them. There's no reason atheist groups can't do it, too.

Offering up group leaders to speak at after-school meetings is another way to let young atheists know there are secular leaders in their community. That works the other way around, too—let the high school students speak to your group about their needs and concerns. And, of course, if your local group is hosting an event or speaker, it would be a great form of outreach to let all high school and college students attend for free.

In addition, local groups can also have a tremendous impact from a distance by donating food, drinks, and money for the student groups, all of which makes a difference when it comes to the number of students willing to attend a meeting and the kinds of events the groups can put on.

The Long, Worthwhile Road Ahead

We're all in this together. It's not easy to be an atheist anywhere, even though things have gotten significantly better over the past few decades. But students have it far worse than the adults do. As adults, if we lose a friend or two when coming out as an atheist, it's not necessarily the end of the world. As teenagers, that's much more devastating. But we're seeing so many ways that atheist student groups and adult allies can enrich their lives. We have to keep that going.

After all this discussion of the problems found in schools and the challenges young atheists face, let's take a moment to celebrate how far we've come over the past few years and talk about where our community could still use some improvement.

9

Graduation

Where We Go from Here

On October 5, 2010, Fox aired an episode of the popular show *Glee* in which character Kurt Hummel comes out as an atheist to his friends. Here's the setup for the scene: After Kurt's father has suffered a heart attack, fellow glee club member Mercedes sings a song with religious overtones to help him deal with the pain. He compliments her singing, but announces that he doesn't believe in God:

> ...I think God is kind of like Santa Claus for adults. Otherwise, God's kind of a jerk, isn't he? I mean, he makes me gay and has his followers going around telling me it's something that I chose. As if someone would choose to be mocked every single day of their life. And right now, I don't want a heavenly father. I want my real one back.

When Mercedes reacts negatively, challenging Kurt to prove that God does not exist, he challenges her right back:

> You can't *prove* that there isn't a magic teapot floating around on the dark side of the moon with a dwarf inside of it that reads romance novels and shoots lightning out of its boobs, but it seems pretty unlikely, doesn't it?

What made this dialogue so fascinating wasn't just that a show's main character was an atheist; it's that he was portrayed as a *likable* one, giving voice to thoughts that thousands of other atheists have shared, on one of the most popular primetime shows in America. While other fictional atheists have appeared on television before, most of them—like Dr. Perry Cox on *Scrubs* and Dr. Gregory House on *House M.D.*—have not been very pleasant.

Maybe we shouldn't be all that surprised. As more atheists begin to make themselves known, they're far less likely to be demonized when compared to previous generations. In the process, they're becoming more acceptable to the general public.

Fifty years ago, this was almost unthinkable.

A Gallup poll from 1958 asked Americans whether they would consider voting for a qualified member of their political party to be President if that person were also an atheist. At the time, only 18 percent of Americans answered, "Yes," making "atheist" the least popular option on the list. (By way of comparison, 38 percent of Americans said they would vote for a black person, 54 percent said they would vote for a woman, and 67 percent said they would vote for a Catholic.)

However, when Gallup asked the same question to Americans in 2012, the responses were markedly different. This time, the percentage of Americans willing to vote for an atheist had *tripled* to 54 percent. "Atheist" was still the least popular option, but it finally garnered a small majority of support.[1]

That wasn't the only bit of surprising news. When Gallup broke down the responses by age group, the results were astonishing. While only 40 percent of Americans sixty-five or older said they would vote for an atheist, the number rose to 70 percent for those in the eighteen to twenty-nine age group. In short, the vast majority of *young* Americans had no problem voting for a qualified atheist from their party. There's no reason to think the percentage has reached its peak, either. While there's still a lot of room for growth, it's no longer unreasonable to think we will see more atheists running for higher office in the future—and winning their seats.

The only way this trend will continue, though, is if atheists don't keep their non-theistic identities to themselves.

The more atheists we have willing to stand up for their rights, the easier our fights will become. They need to go public with their atheism and they need to fight back when religious groups and individuals try to tear down the wall of separation between church and state.

Andrew Seidel, the FFRF attorney, has a vision of what the future could look like if this happens:

> In ten years, we will probably be fighting many of the same cases, but fewer of them. And given the shifting demographics, we will win cases a lot more frequently without having to go to court. A complaint letter will be all that's needed for the schools to stop their illegal actions. Social acceptance of atheists will make things easier for everybody.[2]

That's a lot easier said than done. For many students, realizing that they don't believe in God marks the first time they're acknowledging that their parents (and pastors and teachers) are *wrong* about something so significant. It's very unnerving to think that just about all the adults in your life have been leading you down the wrong path (in your opinion) and it forces you to second-guess many of the other nuggets of information they've taught you up until that point.

That same thought, however, can be very inspirational. For students to know that they came to their own conclusions about something as serious as religion, and that they can back up their arguments and point to evidence contradicting everybody else... that's a powerful moment in the life of any young atheist.

But it doesn't automatically mean they're ready to tell their friends about it.

Even atheists who go to college aren't always eager to let others know they don't believe in God. For high school students, it's even more daunting. David Niose, the author of *Nonbeliever Nation*, explained why:

In high school, the pressure to conform is at its zenith. For a college student to join a Secular Student Alliance group, it's relatively easy, but a high school student may have to deal with significant pressures. They're still living at home, subject to their parents' rules, and that can make it tough for an atheist student—at least one whose parents are religious—to openly identify as atheist, much less join an atheist club. This is why they need support and information.[3]

Still, Niose is optimistic. In ten years, he predicts a landscape that is much more welcoming for secular students, wherever they may live.

In order to make that a reality, we need more students willing to risk their social stock by calling out their teachers and administrators when they push their religious beliefs into places where they have no business being. We also need students willing to be leaders for the secular community on their campus.

Think of what could happen if more young atheists asserted themselves:

- Imagine a classroom where half the students didn't stand for the Pledge of Allegiance.

- Imagine a public school assembly featuring a proselytizing Christian group and a large group of students walking out in protest.

- Imagine atheist students running for student body president—and winning. Imagine those same students running for Congress ten to twenty years down the road.

- Imagine a school newspaper featuring a column (or letter-to-the-editor) about the need for more evolution education in science class, or the benefits of reading more modern books in English class even if they contain adult language and situations, or the reasons to adopt a comprehensive sex ed curriculum—all written from a non-religious perspective.

- Imagine a freshman orientation where, in addition to booths for the Model United Nations, chess team, and Orchesis, there is also a booth for the school's Secular Student Alliance.

- Imagine the majority of students on an athletic team approaching the principal because their coach wrongly led them in a prayer before a big game.

- Imagine if teachers who used the classroom to advance their religious beliefs were challenged by multiple students demanding evidence for the teachers' claims.

- Imagine if every administrator cared more about preventing prejudice and proselytization in their buildings than saving kids from an imagined eternal damnation.

This is all within the realm of possibility. And none of these things require all the students in question to be atheists, either. We need religious allies to stand up for the rights of young atheists just as much as we need atheist students speaking up for themselves.

The Secular Student Alliance's former high school specialist JT Eberhard put the impetus for social change on atheists who remained silent about their non-belief:

No matter how good you think your situation is, it could be better. You deserve better and you're almost certainly legally entitled to it. We can hide in the closet to make things easier for ourselves, letting others make us ashamed for who we are, but it won't change things for the other students. Things are bad now because previous generations didn't speak up. You may lose some friends in the process, but you'll be making a difference for people you've never even met. And you can bet there are people waiting to love you for who you are.[4]

Even though there are high schools all across the country where openly non-religious students are few or non-existent, that's changing thanks to the current crop of atheist activists. As atheists assert their presence in America, we can be assured that we're never going back to a time when any given student is the *only* atheist in his/her school or community. The question is whether those students have the opportunity and courage to say that out loud.

We can make that a reality.

Taking Caution as More Young Atheists Emerge

After an entire book talking about the need for atheists to come out and form groups and the need for adults to help them, I should acknowledge some of the major concerns about the rise of young atheists.

One concern is that we're insensitive to religious students. This goes beyond the question of "what's true?" It suggests that we're creating atheist activists who are so focused on advancing their own beliefs that they don't acknowledge the struggles many religious students (usually the ones not in the majority) have to face. When it comes to young people, shouldn't we be supporting activism that encourages open conversation and religious dialogue instead of trying to answer questions of who's right and who's wrong?

Chris Mooney was an intern at the Center for Inquiry, a non-profit group that advocates for a secular society, in 1998. He has since gone on to write a string of best-selling books, including *The Republican War on Science*. As one of the co-founders of a secular student group at Yale University, he has experience as a group leader. Yet, he told me that he has concerns about campus activism being led by those who tend to see things in black and white. He admits that, if he were in college today, he would've loved that approach, though he no longer believes it's the best one:

> If I was doing it now, I'm really afraid I would've been radicalized by various kinds of activists and turned into something that I don't approve of... the prominent voices that exist now didn't exist when I was doing it and if they had, I know we would have eaten it up.[5]

Mooney does, however, see real value in campus atheist groups when it comes to what else they can offer:

> One of the best goals that I can imagine is to basically provide a support network for people who are trying to figure out who they are... I think that's very valuable... My fear is that there's this whole "Let's do away with religion" thing and "religion is at the root of the world's wrongs"... and I think that's really getting it wrong... You can't do away with religion.

I share Mooney's concern. There's a real fear I have that many older activists want to support student groups that essentially tell students "God doesn't exist" instead of giving them the tools to figure that out for themselves. In that sense, we're not always different from the churches we rail against. I would hope that conversion (or de-conversion, as it were) is not the predominant goal of high school atheist groups and adult allies. Atheist clubs at that age should provide a safe space to talk about religious doubt and question religious assumptions. They should be focused on the journey instead of the destination. They should want to change the prevailing stereotypes against atheists, not pigeonhole all religious people into the same mold.

From personal experience, I have seen many speakers and writers work off of the assumption that God doesn't exist. I do it on my own blog, too. But when we're working with students who are only beginning to realize their non-religious convictions, it would be worthwhile to not hand them the answers we believe are true. They need to figure this out on their own. We would serve them well by posing more questions instead of just offering our own rebuttals.

Eric Snyder, who helped co-found the Secular Student Alliance, shares a different concern about the future of the movement: It's too myopic. Creating campus groups at colleges and high school is a great *first* step, he says, but what good is it if you can't harness all the students to transform the world? He sees a lot of sideways motion—student activists finding different ways to tear down religion—but not enough climbing up the staircase. Eric believes we need to find better ways of creating future leaders, educators, and organizers—a way to think beyond the "typical atheist canon of concerns."

There is a golden opportunity right now for young atheists to do that. Most campus groups I've seen spend a lot of time organizing debates on God's existence and bringing in speakers who can eloquently knock down the "evidence" offered by religious apologists. If only that same amount of energy could be used to sponsor blood drives, coordinate volunteers to go to local soup kitchens, and to raise money for charity. (Some groups have indeed done these things, but many more could stand to include community service in their roster of activities.)

Not everyone is going to graduate from school and become a full-time activist. Atheists go into any number of fields and we should help them be vocal advocates of evidence-based research, good science, and equal rights for everybody no matter what line of work they go into. It's easy to tear down religion, but secular groups of all ages could do so much more to showcase their Humanism and their dedication to ethics and justice without resorting to religion.

Certainly, at the high school level, an atheist group could easily be focused on Humanism in action. In fact, that would make it much more difficult for an administrator to block the group from forming... and much more embarrassing if the story hit the press.

Now's the Time for Young Atheists to Take Action

Concerns noted, it's now up to young atheists to take control of their identities. Many atheists have been silent for too long and we've all paid a price for it. High school students can change that—they can transform their classmates' perceptions of atheists before the stereotypes take over and they grow up fearful of the non-religious. They can spread reason to their classmates before they are in positions to pass laws based on misguided religious beliefs. The rest of us can support those atheist students. It's not enough for a few individuals to take the lead on this; this must be a revolution that involves students everywhere speaking up, speaking out, and creating communities for their peers.

It starts by seeking out allies among your family members, friends, and community. They may not all agree with your beliefs but hopefully most support your right to not believe in God and be open about that.

It involves reading both the classic and popular literature on atheism in order to educate yourself on issues relating to atheism. Sam Harris, Richard Dawkins, Christopher Hitchens, Ayaan Hirsi Ali, and Daniel Dennett have all written extensively on the problems with religion and religious beliefs, and their arguments are worth knowing when a religious students looks to debate with you. At the same time, people like Thomas Jefferson, Roger Williams, and James Madison had a lot to say about the need for church/state separation around the time our country was founded. Their writing offers a historic basis for how our nation ought to be governed and can help support your arguments for freedom *of* religion as well as freedom *from* religion.

Of course, I would also recommend finding atheist blogs that resonate with you, and reading and commenting on them. But it's not enough to just read other people's blogs. You should consider starting your own. (And, if you feel comfortable with it, use your real name.)

That also means sharing your opinions about religion with the people close to you, in person and on social networking websites like Facebook and Twitter.

For some, that could mean posting videos on YouTube where you talk about your atheism and what it means to you.

Whatever you do, find a way to share your thoughts with the world. You never know how many people you might be helping. Not everybody has the luxury to do this, but if you're one of the lucky people whose livelihood and relationships won't be ruined by your public admission of atheism, you ought to take advantage of that.

By the way, if you or your atheist group do anything you feel ought to be shared with the wider public, I would love to post about it on my website. My email address is Mpromptu@gmail.com. (Really. It's the same email address my mom uses for me.) Let me know if you have any questions about what you read in this book, stories you want to share, or events your group put together. I can't wait to hear them.

Epilogue

For those wondering how Nicole Smalkowski is doing now, there's good news. Her family eventually filed a lawsuit against the Hardesty Public School District. In 2008, the case was settled and the school district paid the family an undisclosed sum of money.[1] Her family eventually moved out of Oklahoma. While she no longer plays basketball, Nicole has launched a music career. She released her first album, "Louder," in 2010 under the stage name Niki Ski.[2] She now lives in Tennessee.

Jessica Ahlquist's life has taken a different turn as well. Instead of heading back to Cranston High School West for her senior year, she decided to study with a private tutor instead. Not only will she avoid further unwanted attention at school, she'll have the opportunity to travel and speak about what she went through and why it was worth fighting for. Jessica still has a close-knit group of friends from school. She had always been a quiet and reserved young woman and her ordeal didn't win her many new friends at school, but a few classmates supported her before the case went to court and they've remained close over the past couple of years. What Jessica appreciates more than anything, she says, is how the atheist community didn't just give her awards; they treated her like a close friend. When she won the lawsuit, the Secular Student Alliance sent Jessica a box of ice cream[3] and the bloggers at Skepchick.org sent her cupcakes. "That's not just a professional 'Feel better'," Jessica said. "That's what friends do for each other."

She has also become a hero to a number of older atheists who call her an "evil little thing" out of admiration instead of anger. Jessica couldn't be happier, telling me, "I wouldn't ever want to go back to what I had before."[4]

She's still undecided about her college plans.

Appendix

"Thoughts For Atheists at Graduation"

By Edwin Kagin, National Legal Director and former Kentucky State Director for American Atheists

Good evening Sinners.

At high school graduations throughout our country, it is customary for older people to tell younger people what the older people were told by older people, who are now probably dead people, at their own high school baccalaureates and graduations. This is usually some sad, emotional, and boring commentary on how the world and the future is yours, how you are the future, that we are leaving it to you, and that the speaker's generation messed up the world, but the future is still full of limitless possibilities, and that it is up to you to straighten it all out for the generations to come, and that with hard work, faith, and god's help it can all be done.[1]

There, I have just summarized every known high school graduation speech.

When you are old you can tell the same rubbish to a new generation of bright-eyed graduates ready to go forth into the world to breed, grow old, and die. The problem with all of these far-too-long and whining baccalaureate and graduation speeches, or sermons, is that they usually call for more of what has caused the problems complained of. The baccalaureate talks are the worst. That is where educated adults, who should know better, pray to invisible imaginary friends for wished-for things that never happen.

What is wonderful and different tonight is that this is an atheist baccalaureate. And it may be the first such in the history of the United States. So you will go down in history. Some will say you will go to Hell.

As atheists, you know that the world is not run by magic and magical thinking. Atheists do not bring up their children in a land of make believe. We have tried to teach you the principles of reason, critical thinking, logical fallacy, ethical behavior, and the methods of science and evidence. We want you to know that there is a big difference between "righteousness" and "self-righteousness." We want you to know and understand the difference between belief and proof, between faith and fact.

We want you to know that you are part of a great historic tradition of bringing light unto darkness; that there is a difference between that which is ethical and that which is expedient; a difference between being truly moral and being a follower of religious rules. We want you to know that science is based on facts, not on fairy tales. That evolution is a fact and that "Creationism" is a fairy tale; that there is a difference between coincidence and causation; a difference between potential and actual; that an egg is not a chicken and that an acorn is not an oak tree.

At this rite of passage, we want you, our children who are our future, to understand that what happens to each of us, and to our world, is based on cause-and-effect, not on faith and miracles. We want you to know that behavior has consequences. If you run on a wet trail you can slip and be hurt. If you let fools be your rulers, you will be ruled by fools. We want you to live—not for life after death, but for life before death.

We all share the mystery of having been born human. As humans, we are many races, many nations, and many religions. We can learn to live together or we can destroy ourselves. No god is going to save us. We must save ourselves.

For your own safety's sake, we have tried to help you learn to distinguish between logic and fallacy; between science and superstition; between real and pretend; between the wonder of discovery and magical thinking. We want you to know the difference between doing and dogma; between imagination and mythology. And we want you to understand that learning never ends. We want you to know, as many do not, that life does not stop with high school graduation.

None of us know the limits of what you may yet learn and what you may yet become. There will also be some pain and some disappointments. It is all part of the deal. We did not make the rules.

Most importantly, we want to help you, our children, who are now young adults, to be competent.

You will be competent when you can survive, thrive, create, empathize, and interact justly with others, free of pain, fear, and guilt—without gods, without religion, and without us.

If you can achieve, as we know you can, self-reliant adulthood, you will not need the gods or the religion, and you will not miss them. If we have done it right, you will not need us either.

But perhaps you will miss us.

There is one thing we want. We want you, and your children, and your children's children, to be able to live in a world where it is okay not to believe in god. To do otherwise is to defile the graves of our martyrs.

May your future be better than your past, and may that measure of peace, justice, harmony, and understanding that is denied to religion and its deities, be attained by you as mortals through the use of your minds; and may reason, science, curiosity, and discovery replace the fear, the guilt, the pain, and the ignorance of trembling in terror before capricious gods.

Resources

These are the resources that would have been indispensable to me when I was in high school. If you haven't experienced them already, I strongly recommend them.

The God Delusion by Richard Dawkins. This book offers the ultimate arguments against God's existence. Arguably the best-selling atheist book of all time, it is easy to understand.

Atheism for Dummies by Dale McGowan. This introduction to atheism not only covers thousands of years of freethought history, it also deals with other aspects of being non-religious (like the meaning of life, death, and what the modern atheist movement looks like).

Letting Go of God by Julia Sweeney. This is a funny and beautiful one-woman show about how the author went from wanting to become a nun to eventually not believing in God at all.

The Skeptic's Annotated Bible (http://skepticsannotatedbible.com/). This website and book highlight every instance of injustice, intolerance, and cruelty in the Bible, Quran, and Book of Mormon.

.Reddit Atheism (http://www.reddit.com/r/atheism/). This website is a collection of serious stories, funny images, current events, and interesting comments, all from an atheist perspective. A constant source of insight and laughter.

Notes

Chapter 1: The Outcasts

1 John Stossel, Sylvia Johnson, and Lynn Redmond, "The Black Sheep of Hardesty," ABC News, May 11, 2007, <http://abcnews.go.com/2020/story?id=3164811&page=1&singlePage=true>

2 Ibid.

3 Caroline Mala Corbin, "Nonbelievers and Government Religious Speech" (March 28, 2011), *Iowa Law Review*, Vol. 97, 2011. Available at SSRN: http://ssrn.com/abstract=1797804.

4 *Smalkowski v. Hardesty Public School District,* No. CIV-06-845-M (2006).

5 Stossel, Johnson, and Redmond, "The Black Sheep of Hardesty."

6 Corbin, "Nonbelievers and Government Religious Speech."

7 http://www.democraticunderground.com/discuss/duboard.php?az=show_messg&forum=173&topic_id=1263&mesg_id=1510 (Charleyski, Reply to *It's Even Worse if You Are a Liberal and Have No Gods,* DEMOCRATIC UNDERGROUND, Dec. 09, 2005, 5:56 A.M.

8 Ibid.

9 Ibid.

10 Stossel, Johnson, and Redmond, "The Black Sheep of Hardesty."

11 *Smalkowski v. Hardesty Public School District.*

12 http://youtu.be/npqbgBHYSKk.

13 http://abcnews.go.com/2020/story?id=3164811&page=1&singlePage=true.

14 Katherine Stewart, *The Good News Club: The Christian Right's Stealth Assault on America's Children*, (New York: PublicAffairs, 2012), 218.

15 http://youtu.be/SSyMnUN_jwE.

16 http://atheism.about.com/b/2010/12/10/cranston-high-school-prayer-banner.htm.

17 http://www.riaclu.org/documents/CranstonschoolprayerdisplayletterJuly62010.pdf.

18 http://jessicaahlquist.com/2011/05/a-quick-history/.

19 http://news.providencejournal.com/breaking-news/2011/03/cranston-schools-and-aclu-to-g.html.

20 http://www.becketfund.org/ahlquist-v-city-of-cranston-rhode-island-2011-present/.

21 http://www.riaclu.org/documents/Ahlquistv.CranstonComplaint.pdf.

22 http://www.patheos.com/blogs/friendlyatheist/2011/10/11/jessica-ahlquist-on-the-front-page-of-the-providence-journal/.
23 http://www.facebook.com/groups/179298715436387/.
24 *Ahlquist v. Cranston*, No. 1:11-cv-00138-L-DLM (2012).
25 http://jesusfetusfajitafishsticks.blogspot.com/2012/01/ahlquist-screenshots-if-by-christian.html.
26 http://news.providencejournal.com/breaking-news/2012/01/photo-all-seems.html.
27 http://news.providencejournal.com/breaking-news/2012/01/cranston-police-24.html.
28 http://630wpro.com/Article.asp?id=2371375&spid=18074.
29 Not long after being called out on it, Moura deleted her @Senator_B_Moura Twitter account. However, she has since created a new one: @BethyLM.
30 http://www.evillittleshirts.com/.
31 http://www.patheos.com/blogs/friendlyatheist/2012/01/20/cranston-florists-dont-want-to-do-business-with-atheists/.
32 http://www.nytimes.com/2012/01/27/us/rhode-island-city-enraged-over-school-prayer-lawsuit.html.
33 http://www.npr.org/2012/02/14/146538958/rhode-island-district-weighs-students-prayer-lawsuit.
34 http://abcnews.go.com/US/rhode-island-teens-battle-prayer-banner-mayor/story?id=15386786#.T9oUeitYsdQ.

Chapter 2: Taking Attendance

1
http://www.hhs.gov/ohrp/humansubjects/guidance/belmont.html#xbenefit.
2 http://www.gallup.com/poll/147887/Americans-Continue-Believe-God.aspx.
3 The actual data says 59-64, not 50-64. I am assuming this was a typo.
4 http://commons.trincoll.edu/aris/publications/aris-2008-summary-report/.
5 http://commons.trincoll.edu/aris/publications/american-nones-the-profile-of-the-no-religion-population/.
6 http://commons.trincoll.edu/aris/files/2011/08/NONES_08.pdf.
7 http://www.pewforum.org/Age/Religion-Among-the-Millennials.aspx.
8
http://www.pewforum.org/uploadedFiles/Topics/Demographics/Age/millennials-report.pdf.
9 http://www.patheos.com/blogs/friendlyatheist/2012/10/09/new-report-a-third-of-adults-under-30-have-no-religious-affiliation/.

10

http://www.pewforum.org/uploadedFiles/Topics/Religious_Affiliation/Unaf
filiated/NonesOnTheRise-full.pdf.
[11] http://www.people-press.org/2012/06/04/section-6-religion-and-social-
values/.
[12] http://www.people-press.org/files/legacy-pdf/06-04-
12%20Values%20Release.pdf.
[13] http://publicreligion.org/research/2012/04/millennial-values-survey-
2012/.
[14] http://publicreligion.org/site/wp-content/uploads/2012/04/Millennials-
Survey-Report.pdf.
[15] http://www.people-press.org/2007/01/09/a-portrait-of-generation-
next/.
[16] http://www.people-press.org/files/legacy-pdf/300.pdf.
[17] http://thehumanist.org/july-august-2012/nonbeliever-nation-the-rise-of-
secular-americans/.

Chapter 3: The Principal's Office
[1] *Widmar v. Vincent,* 454 U.S. 263 (1981).
[2] http://blog.speakupmovement.org/university/freedom-of-speech/the-
story-behind-widmar-v-vincent/.
[3] http://www.law.cornell.edu/uscode/text/20/4071.
    [4] *Larry L. McSwain and William Loyd Allen,* Twentieth-Century Shapers of
    Baptist Social Ethics *(Mercer University Press, 2008), 290.*

[5] http://www.ffrf.org/legacy/fttoday/1996/nov96/butler.html.
[6] http://www.law2.byu.edu/lawreview/archives/1986/2/woo.pdf.
[7] http://www2.ed.gov/policy/elsec/guid/secletter/110607.html.
[8] http://www.people.com/people/archive/article/0,,20118060,00.html.
9
http://caselaw.lp.findlaw.com/scripts/getcase.pl?court=US&vol=496&invol=
226.
[10] Email to author, July 2, 2012.
[11] http://www.patheos.com/blogs/friendlyatheist/2009/02/28/high-school-
student-faces-challenges-in-starting-an-atheist-group/.
12
http://www.reddit.com/r/atheism/comments/f7vrd/so_i_tried_to_start_a_se
cular_student_club_at_my/.
[13] http://freethoughtblogs.com/wwjtd/2012/06/06/my-work-with-the-ssa/.
[14] Email correspondence with author, June 26, 2012.
[15] http://www.patheos.com/blogs/friendlyatheist/2011/04/21/junior-high-
atheist-talks-about-his-segment-on-nick-news/.

[16] http://www.patheos.com/blogs/friendlyatheist/2012/06/05/at-a-texas-high-school-saying-atheist-could-disrupt-the-learning-process/.
[17] Email correspondence with author, June 22, 2012.
[18] http://ffrf.org/legacy/fttoday/1996/may96/butler.html.
[19] http://ffrf.org/legacy/fttoday/1996/may96/club.html.
[20] http://ffrf.org/legacy/fttoday/1996/may96/butler.html.
[21] http://ffrf.org/legacy/fttoday/1996/nov96/butler.html.
[22] http://ffrf.org/legacy/fttoday/1996/nov96/butler.html.
[23] http://ffrf.org/legacy/fttoday/2000/jan_feb2000/white.html.
[24] http://www.washingtonpost.com/national/on-faith/not-just-chess-atheists-are-organizing-high-school-clubs-too/2012/06/29/gJQAaBPmBW_story.html.

Chapter 4: Peer Pressure
[1] http://www.patheos.com/blogs/friendlyatheist/2010/10/14/whats-it-like-running-a-high-school-atheist-group/.
[2] http://articles.chicagotribune.com/2007-06-27/news/0706270147_1_first-year-camper-nature-hikes-atheists/2.
[3] Conversation with author, July 7, 2012.
[4] Conversation with author, July 7, 2012.
[5] http://www.gallup.com/poll/147662/first-time-majority-americans-favor-legal-gay-marriage.aspx.
[6] http://www.patheos.com/blogs/friendlyatheist/2012/06/07/high-school-student-fights-to-stay-seated-during-the-pledge-of-allegiance-and-wins/.
[7] Email with author June 11, 2012.
[8] http://philadelphia.cbslocal.com/2012/06/06/collingswood-student-fights-for-her-right-to-stay-seated-during-pledge-of-allegiance/.
[9] Email with author, July 7, 2012.
[10]
http://www.reddit.com/r/atheism/comments/hed7y/threatened_to_contact_aclu_for_prayer_at/.
[11] http://www.patheos.com/blogs/friendlyatheist/2011/05/20/this-district-is-about-to-get-sued/.
[12] http://www.bastropenterprise.com/features/x2132687894/Student-challenges-prayer-at-Bastrop-graduation.
[13] http://www.bastropenterprise.com/features/x2132687894/Student-challenges-prayer-at-Bastrop-graduation.
[14] http://au.org/blogs/wall-of-separation/damon%E2%80%99s-contribution-louisiana-graduate-stands-up-for-constitution-%E2%80%93-and.
[15] http://www.patheos.com/blogs/friendlyatheist/2011/05/20/this-district-is-about-to-get-sued/

[16] http://www.tolerance.org/magazine/number-40-fall-2011/unaffiliated-unite.

[17] http://www.patheos.com/blogs/friendlyatheist/2011/05/21/what-happened-at-damon-fowlers-graduation/.

[18] Readers of my website raised over $30,000 toward a college scholarship for Damon.

[19] http://www.patheos.com/blogs/friendlyatheist/2012/05/19/damon-fowlers-legacy-no-prayer-at-his-former-high-schools-graduation-this-time-around/.

[20] Email to author, July 4, 2012..

[21] Ibid.

[22] http://www.patheos.com/blogs/friendlyatheist/2011/04/16/christian-complains-about-atheist-students-at-a-high-school/.

[23] http://www.patheos.com/blogs/friendlyatheist/2011/05/06/parent-removes-children-from-school-because-atheists-set-up-table-during-lunch/.

Chapter 5: The Morning Bell

[1] http://caselaw.lp.findlaw.com/scripts/getcase.pl?navby=CASE&court=US&vol=374&page=203.

[2] http://nationaldayofprayer.org/news/news-releases/news-release-may-2-2012/.

[3] http://en.wikisource.org/wiki/Public_Law_83-396.

[4] http://www.usmint.gov/about_the_mint/fun_facts/?action=fun_facts5.

[5] http://www.treasury.gov/about/education/Pages/in-god-we-trust.aspx.

[6] http://www.secularstudents.org/node/403.

[7] Email to author, July 26, 2012.

[8] http://ffrf.org/publications/freethought-today/articles/A-Champion-of-the-First-Amendment/.

[9] http://aclupa.blogspot.com/2006/12/guest-blogger-ellery-schempp.html.

[10] http://en.wikipedia.org/wiki/Abington_School_District_v._Schempp.

[11] http://www.secularstudents.org/node/403.

[12] http://ffrf.org/publications/freethought-today/articles/A-Champion-of-the-First-Amendment/.

[13] http://www.ffrf.org/legal/challenges/indianapolis-public-schools-changes-discriminatory-internet-filtering-policy/.

[14] http://www.ffrf.org/legal/challenges/ffrf-unblocks-atheist-websites-from-san-antonio-isd-filter-feb-16-2012/.

[15] http://ffrf.org/uploads/legal/HoustonCountyGA%232.pdf.

[16] http://ffrf.org/legal/challenges/virginia-school-removes-ten-commandments/.

[17] Email to author, July 10, 2012

.*18 Andrew C. Revkin, "Devoted Fly Their Message to Graduates God's in Air at Religion-Free Rite" [Valley Edition] Los Angeles Times, 19 June 1986.*

19 "Atheist wins ban on prayer," *Ludington Daily News,* June 5, 1986.

20 http://onlineathens.com/stories/061299/ope_ThomasCol.shtml.

21 Lyndsey Layton, "Nick Becker Wanted a High School Diploma Without the Prayer. He Ended Up With a Reputation." *The Washington Post* June 22, 1999. http://www.washingtonpost.com/wp-srv/style/features/becker062299.htm.

22 http://www.scribd.com/doc/28255503/Workman-v-Grenwood-Complt.

23 http://ffrf.org/publications/freethought-today/articles/the-indiana-student-who-stopped-school-prayer/.

24 http://www.patheos.com/blogs/friendlyatheist/2010/05/25/greenwood-high-school-tries-to-circumvent-injunction-against-graduation-prayer/.

25 http://www.patheos.com/blogs/friendlyatheist/2010/05/29/how-did-greenwood-high-schools-graduation-go/#comment-482512.

26 http://www.theindychannel.com/news/23693748/detail.html.

27 http://www.patheos.com/blogs/friendlyatheist/2010/05/30/eric-workmans-graduation-speech/.

28 http://www.theindychannel.com/video/23716117/index.html.

29 http://ffrf.org/publications/freethought-today/articles/the-indiana-student-who-stopped-school-prayer/.

30 Conversation with author, July 23, 2012.

31 http://www.patheos.com/blogs/friendlyatheist/2010/05/29/how-did-greenwood-high-schools-graduation-go/.

32 http://www.patheos.com/blogs/friendlyatheist/2011/05/14/high-school-student-puts-a-stop-to-graduation-prayer-vote/.

33 http://www.ffrf.org/outreach/awards/student-activist-awards/harrison-hopkins1/.

34 http://www.firstamendmentschools.org/freedoms/case.aspx?id=489.

35 http://ffrf.org/publications/freethought-today/articles/football-prayers-are-offensive-lines-for-nonbelievers/.

36 http://www.timesfreepress.com/news/2010/oct/20/national-group-demands-end-prayers-soddy-daisy-hig/?local.

37 http://au.org/blogs/wall-of-separation/sorry-soddy-daisy-public-schools-should-not-promote-one-faith-over-others.

38 http://ffrf.org/publications/freethought-today/articles/football-prayers-are-offensive-lines-for-nonbelievers/.

39 http://ffrf.org/uploads/legal/RidgelandHighSchool,GAfootballviolations.pdf.

40 http://ffrf.org/uploads/legal/RidgelandHigh%20School,GA%232LCofferand Chaplainw:outRICOcomplaint.pdf.

41
http://www.patheos.com/blogs/friendlyatheist/2009/10/02/cheerleaders-bible-banners-banned-from-football-games/.
42 http://www.patheos.com/blogs/friendlyatheist/2009/10/27/update-on-the-cheerleaders%E2%80%99-banned-bible-banners/.
43
http://www.patheos.com/blogs/friendlyatheist/2012/09/19/cheerleaders-at-texas-high-school-angry-because-they-cant-hold-up-biblical-run-through-signs-at-football-games/.
44
http://ffrf.org/uploads/legal/MercedesTX,TeacherCmmtsandNativity%20.pdf.
45 http://www.patheos.com/blogs/friendlyatheist/2011/09/15/math-teacher-with-godly-banners-in-classroom-loses-lawsuit/.
46 http://www.ca9.uscourts.gov/datastore/opinions/2011/09/13/10-55445.pdf.
47 Email to author, September 1, 2012.
48 http://ffrf.org/publications/freethought-today/articles/Sixth-Grader-Proselytized-in-Music-Class/.
49 http://ffrf.org/uploads/legal/HoustonCountyGA-VeteransHSGrad.Prayer.pdf.
50 Email to author, March 24, 2012.
51 Interview with author, July 30, 2012.
52 http://www.aclu-de.org/news/high-school-changes-choral-program-to-respect-religious-freedom/2011/08/15/.
53 http://www.aclu.org/files/assets/anderson_complaint_filed.pdf.
54 http://www.aclu.org/files/assets/anderson_complaint_filed.pdf.
55 http://www.nytimes.com/2011/12/28/us/battling-anew-over-the-place-of-religion-in-public-schools.html?_r=2&pagewanted=all.
56 http://youtu.be/OroiFsPhEpk.
57 http://www.aclu.org/religion-belief/south-carolina-school-district-agrees-stop-proselytizing-students.
58 http://blogs.reuters.com/great-debate/2012/01/25/how-religion-is-infiltrating-public-schools/.

Chapter 6: Homework
1 http://ffrf.org/publications/freethought-today/articles/You-Belong-In-Hell/.
2 http://www.nytimes.com/2006/12/18/nyregion/18kearny.html.
3 http://www.citmedialaw.org/legal-guide/new-jersey/new-jersey-recording-law.
4 http://www.nytimes.com/2006/12/18/nyregion/18kearny.html.

[5] http://ffrf.org/publications/freethought-today/articles/You-Belong-In-Hell/.

[6] http://ffrf.org/publications/freethought-today/articles/You-Belong-In-Hell/.

[7] http://ffrf.org/publications/freethought-today/articles/You-Belong-In-Hell/.

[8] http://www.nytimes.com/2006/12/18/nyregion/18kearny.html.

[9] http://www.nytimes.com/2006/12/31/opinion/nyregionopinions/NJteacher.html.

[10] http://ffrf.org/publications/freethought-today/articles/You-Belong-In-Hell/.

[11] http://www.nytimes.com/2007/02/21/nyregion/21kearny.html.

[12] http://www.nytimes.com/2007/05/10/nyregion/10kearny.html.

[13] http://ffrf.org/publications/freethought-today/articles/You-Belong-In-Hell/.

[14] http://www.annistonstar.com/view/full_story/6753350/article-Alexandria-HS-stops-morning-prayers-after-student-complains?instance=home_lead_story.

[15] Conversation with author, July 7, 2012.

[16] http://www.patheos.com/blogs/friendlyatheist/2011/03/27/putting-a-stop-to-a-public-school-preacher/

[17] http://www.patheos.com/blogs/friendlyatheist/2007/09/20/shes-not-requesting-attention-but-itll-follow-her-anyway/.

[18] http://www.patheos.com/blogs/friendlyatheist/2011/03/26/study-shows-anti-atheist-prejudice-goes-down-when-our-numbers-go-up/.

[19] *Personality and Social Psychology Bulletin* (April 2011 37: 543-556).

[20] http://www.knoxnews.com/news/2012/feb/23/lenoir-city-high-school-wont-publish-atheist-on/.

[21] http://www.knoxnews.com/news/2012/feb/26/krystal-myers-school-promotes-religion-and-of/.

[22] http://www.wilsoncountynews.com/article.php?id=14969&n=teen-scene-respect-the-choice-not-to-believe.

[23] Email to author, July 8, 2012.

[24] Conversation with author, July 7, 2012.

[25] http://ffrf.org/publications/freethought-today/articles/Protesting-One-Nation-Under-God-in-the-Pledge-of-Allegiance/.

[26] Conversation with author, July 7, 2012.

[27] http://content.usatoday.com/communities/Religion/post/2011/02/atheists-group-takes-on-high-school-/1#.UBTiezGe4vE.

[28] http://www.youtube.com/watch?v=m2pkPZCR1Yw.

29
http://content.usatoday.com/communities/Religion/post/2011/02/atheists-
group-takes-on-high-school-/1#.UBTiezGe4vE.
30 http://www.youtube.com/watch?v=m2pkPZCR1Yw.

Chapter 7: Curriculum

1 Email to author, June 27, 2012.
2 http://www.secularstudents.org/mediarelations#lte.
3 http://www.patheos.com/blogs/friendlyatheist/2011/10/15/high-school-
atheists-take-part-in-anti-bullying-campaign/.
4 http://www.secularstudents.org/askanatheistday/.
5 Conversation with author, July 7, 2012.
6 http://www.secularstudents.org/groupstartingpacket.

Chapter 8: The PTA

1 http://ffrf.org/legacy/fttoday/1998/march98/chandler.html.
2 http://ffrf.org/legacy/fttoday/1998/march98/chandler.html.
3 http://ffrf.org/legacy/fttoday/1998/march98/chandler.html.
4 http://ffrf.org/legacy/fttoday/1998/march98/chandler.html.
5 http://ffrf.org/legacy/fttoday/1998/march98/chandler.html.
6
http://www.aclualabama.org/News/PressReleases/ReligiousLiberty/02019
6.htm.
7 http://ffrf.org/legacy/fttoday/1998/march98/chandler.html.
8 http://ffrf.org/legacy/fttoday/1998/march98/chandler.html.
9 http://www.economist.com/node/106131.
10 http://www.libertymagazine.org/index.php?id=537.
11 http://www.economist.com/node/106131.
12
http://www.leagle.com/xmlResult.aspx?page=2&xmldoc=19972047985FSup
p1062_11914.xml&docbase=CSLWAR2-1986-2006&SizeDisp=7.
13 http://www.libertymagazine.org/index.php?id=537.
14 http://articles.chicagotribune.com/1999-07-
15/news/9907150146_1_voluntary-prayer-religious-expression-public-
school-prayer.
15 http://www.aclu.org/religion-belief/long-awaited-victory-high-court-
vacates-alabama-decision-allowing-public-school-pray.
16 http://caselaw.findlaw.com/us-11th-circuit/1181490.html.
17 http://www.secularstudents.org/whysecular.
18 http://www.firstamendmentcenter.org/category/religion.
19 Email to author, July 8, 2012.
20 http://www.facebook.com/groups/125531194999/.

[21] http://ffrf.org/publications/freethought-today/articles/high-school-freethinkers-challenge-religion/.

[22] http://www.tolerance.org/magazine/number-40-fall-2011/unaffiliated-unite.

[23] http://www.nytimes.com/2011/04/04/education/04winerip.html?pagewanted=all.

[24] http://www.tolerance.org/magazine/number-40-fall-2011/unaffiliated-unite.

[25] http://en.wikipedia.org/wiki/Kitzmiller_v._Dover_Area_School_District.

[26] http://en.wikipedia.org/wiki/Selman_v._Cobb_County_School_District.

[27] http://www.nytimes.com/2010/03/13/education/13texas.html.

[28] http://www.azpolicy.org/files/14713/downloads/HowToRunForSchoolBoard.pdf.

[29] http://www.amazon.com/Parenting-Beyond-Belief-Raising-Religion/dp/0814474268.

Chapter 9: Graduation

[1] http://www.gallup.com/poll/155285/atheists-muslims-bias-presidential-candidates.aspx.

[2] Conversation with author, July 7, 2012.

[3] Conversation with author, July 7, 2012.

[4] Conversation with author, July 7, 2012.

[5] Phone interview with Chris Mooney, June 19, 2012.

Epilogue

[1] http://www.atheists.org/upload/Smalkowski_settled.pdf.

[2] http://www.nikiskimusic.com/.

[3] https://twitter.com/jessicaahlquist/statuses/159788997290369024.

[4] Email from Jessica Ahlquist to author, June 15, 2012.

Appendix

[1] This speech is reproduced here with permission of Edward Kagin.

CPSIA information can be obtained at www.ICGtesting.com
Printed in the USA
LVOW101215230613

339830LV00009B/331/P